A Step Into DELIVERANCE

A Step Into
DELIVERANCE

Toni Pugh

WINEPRESS PUBLISHING

© 2001 by Toni Pugh. All rights reserved.

Printed in the United States of America.

Packaged by WinePress Publishing, PO Box 428, Enumclaw, WA 98022. The views expressed or implied in this work do not necessarily reflect those of WinePress Publishing. Ultimate design, content, and editorial accuracy of this work is the responsibility of the author(s).

No part of this publication may be reproduced, stored in a retrieval system or transmitted in any way by any means, electronic, mechanical, photocopy, recording or otherwise, without the prior permission of the copyright holder except as provided by USA copyright law.

Unless otherwise noted, all Scriptures are taken from the King James Version of the Bible.

ISBN 1-57921-373-1
Library of Congress Catalog Card Number: 2001087819

Dedicated to Alva, the desire of my heart, and the children. And to Gerald Conedy, the man who told me that he loved me.

ACKNOWLEDGMENTS

Fortunately, I grew up during an era void of MTV, ESPN, BET, and music videos; consequently, our heroes were people within our neighborhood whom we saw on a regular basis. There was the late Mr. Clark, our mailman / realtor; Dr. Gregory and the honorable dentist, Dr. Wilson; the unforgettable Ms. Virginia Bailous and Virginia Bentley who took time from their own families to be Den Mothers to a group of us. There was historian, Mr. Stevenson and music wonder, Marian Crenshaw, and the late William Hunter who were perhaps God's greatest gifts to public education. They touched us. They taught us. They inspired us to push for excellence.

Also, I salute my fifth grade teacher, Ms. Freda (Keighbaum) Brankey, for giving me a love to read and seventh grade teacher, Ms. Catherine Strain, who read excerpts from her own autobiography each Monday morning. It was then that I decreed that I too would one day write a book about my life.

Contents

Preface 9
Foreword 11
1. Drifters and Dreamers 13
2. The Terminated Honeymoon 23
3. Going Home 29
4. Deeper Life 37
5. First Encounter: Jezebel 51
6. Throw Her Down 67
7. The Turning Point 79
8. And They Spoke 85
9. A Woman Scorned 93
10. He That Findeth A Wife 99
11. And He Chose Twelve 107
12. Questions & Answers / Maneuvers 111
13. Pride 125
14. Talking Spirits 135
15. Lust 143
16. Dominion 151
17. Slothfulness 155
18. The Religious Spirit 161
19. The Baby Spirit 171

20. Anniversary Spirit	175
21. Anger	181
22. Witchcraft	185
23. The Cursed Woman: Jezebel	189
24. The Korah/Absalom Spirit	199
25. Soul Ties	207
26. The Sightlessness of Samson	219
Epilogue	227

Preface

The objective of this manuscript is to present an autobiographical account of how God lead me into the casting out of devils' ministry. We've purposely avoided any theological debate on the actual existence of demons, their origin, and final fate, for there are plenty of good books on the subject. Instead, we've sought to enlighten our readers and stimulate a need to adhere to God's Word, while sharing some of my rich intimacies and lessons I've learned while walking with the Lord. Names of individuals receiving deliverance have been changed for the sake of discretion. Otherwise, all accounts are true and actual life experiences.

Foreword

Although Toni Pugh and I have never met in the flesh, we are brothers and have for many years been in the same School of the Holy Spirit. I appreciate his writing this book for it is full of Divine wisdom and Godly advice which will help any Christian and especially those actively engaged in, or exploring, the ministry of deliverance.

One reason that this book is so powerful is Toni's honesty, self-effacing style and willingness to humble himself and share with us his mistakes, failures and continual need of the Holy Spirit's guidance. I have found that I have learned more through my mistakes and failures, than I did from my successes in deliverance. The Lord, it seems, is continually leading us into new and unfamiliar territory and allowing us to encounter new challenges to teach us not only our dependence upon Himself, but His willingness to grant us wisdom and guidance.

I have been involved in ministry and especially deliverance for over thirty years, and I wish I could have learned many of the truths which Toni shares in this book at the beginning of my own attempts at ministry. It might have saved me a lot of time, and helped me avoid similar problems.

I was especially impressed with his explanation of the Jezebellian influence, which I believe every ministry must confront. I know we have had to battle it. A woman once confided to my wife that she wanted to seduce me—but said that it wasn't a normal physical seduction—she wanted my healing anointing, my mantle of authority and to take over our fellowship. Praise God that He allowed her to see the truth before she could cause a problem.

Another area of this book which I appreciated was Toni's presentation of soul-ties. His treatment of the subject is very good, and he covers several of the same points regarding both good, and bad soul-ties which my wife and I cover in our most recent book, *Breaking Unhealthy Soul-Ties*.

The LORD told Habakkuk (Hab. 2:2) to, *"Write the vision and make it plain upon tables, that he may run that readeth it."* I believe that is just what Toni has done. He has provided a roadmap that any pastor or any Christian may follow to avoid many unnecessary detours and diversions in his walk with the Lord.

William D. Banks, President
Impact Christian Books

Chapter 1

DRIFTERS AND DREAMERS

Just how I came to Irvine, California, can only be traced to divine providence. Originally, I was a drama major at Illinois Wesleyan University in Bloomington, Illinois. I had been bitten by the acting bug after a successful year of speech and drama at McKinley High School in Canton, Ohio. Although my interests were diverse, I figured that a career in the entertainment field would be a launching pad into the arena I desired most: worldwide influence.

My stay at Wesleyan was riddled with disappointment. Here I was, an energetic freshman drama major with loads of talent and optimism, only to find main stage acting was unavailable until our sophomore year. The featured drama my freshman year was Lillian Hellman's, "The Little Foxes." I had played the role of Cal, the butler, in full "Steppin' Fetchit" stereotype as the director requested on a Canton Players Guild main stage production, but the idea of paying top tuition at a private university to do the same was appalling. Besides, why couldn't I have a shot at the main male character? Protests were held, meetings with the Dean and the Drama staff proved fruitless and I was my usual vocal, militant self. The play went on with an audience discussion after the closing act, but my hope in a future at Wesleyan had already soured.

By my second year at Wesleyan, I was fed up with the entire environment. Though the academic atmosphere was excellent, I was ill prepared for its intensity. The black population was sparse and disjointed and I was absolutely livid at the Drama department's inability to cater to the needs of black students.

During my casting in a small avant-garde production I received my ticket out of Wesleyan. Effortless leaps across a series of platforms caught the discerning eyes of a retired dance instructor in the audience, prompting her to ask how long I'd been dancing.

"I never took a dance lesson in my life," I replied.

"But you should—you are a dancer," she said, amazed.

I asked where I should study; Wesleyan lacked a dance department.

"Where would you like to study?" she asked.

"California," I responded.

"Then go to Irvine," she said.

Full of adventure, I finished off my sophomore year at Wesleyan, but not before quitting the Drama School and bringing charges of racism against the department. My letter to twenty-four University regents caused quite a stir, but was eventually dismissed and I left in a huff.

Getting into the University of California in Irvine took some doing. I fled Wesleyan with a D grade point average. I withdrew from one class and received an F in two other classes, but had an A in speech. I gave my speech final on "Why I was leaving Wesleyan." Even though I went fifteen minutes over the speech limit, (and we were warned to never do that in her class), the teacher gave me the top grade for my inexorable passion.

When my application to UCI was rejected that summer on the basis of poor grades, I used my usual rhetoric to get my foot in the door. Then came the million dollar question:

"Where are you going to get the money to pay for tuition?" asked the Dean of Admissions.

With a barrage of words, I questioned how an educational institution could deny any red-blooded American student an opportunity for higher learning on a technicality like lack of money. I ended with:

"Do you want to see a 4.0?"

The Dean of Admissions said that the committee would reconsider my application, and after I hung up I said, "Mom, pack my bags, I'm on my way to California."

Five days later I received an admission letter, only a week before school was to begin. I had been accepted to UCI without financial aid, housing, or knowledge of one living soul in Orange County, California.

I traveled for three days by train across the rugged midwestern terrain to arrive in Irvine with a footlocker, three bags, a bed roll and a driving determination to succeed.

The next several weeks were a struggle. I ended up sleeping in a study lounge in the dormitory where I would one day become Resident Assistant. It was always said that California was a place full of drifters and dreamers and Hollywood star wannabes. Admittedly, I possessed a bit of all the above. I did, however, have a strong propensity to remain focused on one single goal until it was completed. I was creative, not crass, disciplined, not deviant, and oh, ever so cocky. I figured that I had as good a chance at making it big in California as anyone else had, despite the overwhelming consensus of the student body, who felt that I'd be a statistic. The Dean of Admissions shared their view.

"You'll never make it," he decreed. "All the way from Ohio without financial aid and you don't know anyone; no room, no board . . . nope, you're history."

The Dean was wrong. I did know someone in California. I knew myself. I knew that I was strong willed and full of tenacity. I knew that I came from a lineage of survivors. As he shook his head in disbelief, I thought to myself, *How dare this man place limitations on me. He doesn't even know me.* I left his office all the more determined to succeed.

After a semester living with a family only two miles from the University, I entered the campus graduate housing while majoring in dance. I lived on a two-hundred-dollar monthly social security check. Near the end of the year, I applied for and got a job as a Resident Assistant. This meant that I would be in charge of a dormitory, monitoring student behavior and planning activities with free room and board as my pay. I was given the Fine Arts dorm named, Prado, and life suddenly became easier. It was good to have a place to sleep and eat. I was tremendously grateful for both, especially a place to eat; and in that place my life would take a dramatic turn.

One sunny Wednesday noon in 1978, I was sitting amid the buzz of laughter and small talk at the cafeteria known as the Commons. I was surrounded by five Christian brothers with whom I had good rapport. Suddenly, a young man walked over to our table carrying a petition, gathering signatures protesting the University's investments in South Africa, which at that time was under apartheid. After his brief explanation, I boldly snatched the pen from his hand, signed it and handed both pen and petition to my friend Ronald who refused, while saying that he believed that Christ was the answer to South Africa.

My roots were steeped deeply in the sixties, an era accented with dark shades, berets, army boots, clenched fists and all the rhetoric that accompanied militancy and black power. If I believed in any cause, it was worth dying for. There was very little middle ground for me; life was to be lived with an unyielding passion—and here I sat among the most insipid group of fellows on the face of the earth. They possessed the quality in men that I loathed most, passivism. Subversion was in my blood and though I had learned to discipline my radical rage into a quiet storm, Ronald's refusal unleashed a time bomb.

"Christ?" I exploded, "It's people like you who allow racism to prevail! You sit back trusting in a white God invented by white people, while black people everywhere suffer under the oppressive hand of racism!"

Gerald, among the five, looked me square in the face and with moistened eyes said softly, "You know, brother, I've developed a deep love for you." I was taken aback. My stick of dynamite was diffused to a single, unlit birthday candle. Never in my entire life have I had a man say that he loved me and certainly not under such circumstances. Dumbfounded, angry and confused, I left the table speechless, without the slightest hint that within forty-eight hours I would be translated out of the kingdom of darkness into the kingdom of light by the power of Calvary.

Gerald had asked me to attend an on-campus Christian fellowship, BASIC (Brothers and Sisters in Christ) many times before, but this particular Friday I surprised everyone by appearing. About thirty students of all races sat in a circle with opened Bibles, listening intently to a Bible lesson. Just why I was there after our blowup at the lunch table can only be attributed to the convicting power of the Holy Spirit.

I had defected from a Baptist upbringing for worldly pursuits as a teen. While I didn't exactly oppose religion, my militant background had hardened me towards Christianity whose God was largely blond and blue eyed. Now I sat among a group who were enshrouded by a peace I knew not of. I left there with every intention of getting it.

I returned to my three-room apartment and wrestled for what seemed like hours under the convicting power of the Holy Spirit. My hope for a future in the entertainment business, my high aspirations for fame and global influence gave me justifiable grounds to resist the call to Calvary, but the Holy Spirit prevailed. I broke through, fell on my knees, repented deeply of my sins and asked Jesus to come into my life. The torment subsided and I was flooded with an unspeakable peace. I fell fast asleep as a soldier would after many days of warfare. When I awakened, I was still at peace, yet bewildered. Was I saved?

The next morning, much as Nicodemus went to Jesus, I went to a dear Christian sister and sheepishly asked her how one would know if they were saved. An intensely private person, I divulged nothing more. Lynetta smiled a Mona Lisa smile and wrote down some scriptures, saying that they would have new meaning to anyone who was saved. As I was about to leave her dorm room, she said, "Just ask Him!"

Seemed too simple. I waited until midnight, read the scriptures and then asked, "Lord, are You in there?" Instantaneously, a shaft of divine light broke through the ceiling of my room and literally slammed against my forehead, splitting into it as a scalpel would. As my forehead separated, I saw what appeared to be hundreds of tiny black dots the size of coffee grains shoot out from my mind at the speed of light, making the noise of a rushing wind. Suddenly I heard God's voice thundering throughout my entire being as the light flooded my soul.

> "Am I in there? All this time you have wanted to know what truth was . . . What real love was. What real friendship was. What reality was . . . What hope was . . . I AM TRUTH. . . . I AM LOVE. . . . I AM FRIENDSHIP . . . I AM REALITY . . . I AM HOPE. . . . All this time you have sought for knowledge—but you know nothing until you know the love of God!"

Now I know how Israel felt at the foot of Sinai as God delivered the Ten Commandments the very first time. My whole being quaked at the sound of His voice. I fell to my knees and wept like a newborn babe. After collecting myself, I stayed up most of the night reading in the Gospel of John. Smitten by its purity, awed by its beauty, I realized for the very first time just how much Jesus loved me.

The next morning I felt a humility which I had never known. I awoke with an awareness of the presence of God for the first time, and I could only respond by raising my arms in worship. After dressing, I headed for the Commons and the first person I saw was Lynetta. I was speechless. She simply smiled and scurried away to class. Upon approaching the Commons, I met the same fellows whom I had cursed only hours before. The change in me was apparent to all. We embraced, cried, and I went joyfully into the cafeteria. For the next several days I behaved like a whipped puppy. The once loquacious, politically-minded rhetorician had met his match. I had been humbled by One greater than I and loved every moment of it.

The word that Toni Pugh had been born again spread throughout the campus like a forest fire on a dry autumn day. A steady stream of well-wishers knocked at my door bearing smiles, congratulations, scriptures, hugs and words of encouragement. Many of them I had never known, until I beheld their radiant faces and felt their outstretched arms.

Their kindness and sincerity reduced me to tears over and over, especially the kindness showed to me by my white brothers. "Toni, here is my number. Call anytime. If you ever need to get off campus just ask. Here are the keys to my car." I could hear the Lord speaking to my heart very gently, "You see My son, there is no black or white in Christ."

One knock on my door yielded a tremendous surprise. On the other side of my door was a Chicano whom I had come close to fighting in the Commons. It all started at a meeting for minority students. A mixture of Chinese, Mexican American, Japanese and African Americans discussed the controversial removal of affirmative action from UC campuses. I was in my usual rare form, speaking things that brought both laughter and applause from everyone except him. He ran me down in the cafeteria the following day and got in my face and called me a racist. With his chest buried against mine, pushing began and a two-minute shouting match attracted a small crowd of on-lookers. I had never seen him again, until now.

He was humble and apologetic and spoke amicably. He told me that he was a born-again believer and had heard the news about my conversion. He shared this scripture with me before we embraced and called one another brother. *"The eyes of the Lord searcheth to and fro throughout the whole earth to show himself strong in the behalf of them whose heart is perfect towards Him"* (II Chronicles 16.8).

The point was clear: God was a God of all races and He was a God of reconciliation. This was a lesson I would learn repeatedly. The grave of racial animosity had been opened by God's amazing grace and the rotting corpse of hate had to be exhumed and destroyed forever. God had to take me into some painful situations before the root of my racial bitterness could finally be dissolved.

As part of my healing, God took me back to my childhood, when I was about eight years old. I was in the third grade at Lathrop Elementary School, horsing around in the hallway as our class went to the library. Edward and I played tag at the back of the line. While dodging his reach, I ran smack into the Principal, who was showing two male visitors the school. I had violated a strict rule and was whisked off to the Principal's office. "I'm going to show you how we discipline our students around here," he said proudly to the guests.

I was told to bend over as the Principal took out an inch thick paddle and slammed it against my backside with what felt like the strength of Hercules. I fell to the floor on both forearms, writhing in pain. Despite my hysteria, he said something else to the visitors, picked me up by my belt and gave me two more harrowing swats. I fell on my face again, screaming in a voice that could be heard outside the office door. Not only had my backside been set ablaze, my spirit had been crushed beyond measure.

Unable to stop crying, they stood me in the corner of an office supply room and later allowed me to lie down. I sobbed myself to sleep, missing the entire afternoon of school. On my way home I continued crying over the injustice. He was merely showing off for those men. He didn't have to hit me like he did. He would never do this to own children. He didn't have to treat me like a dog.

With angry tears, I rehearsed the scene to my mother, but she did nothing. As I sat on the curb with my hands holding my head, I wished I had a father, for certainly he would go get this man who had caused me so much pain and embarrassment. What entered me at that point were spirits of revenge and bitterness and a powerful demon called hate, hatred for white people.

Years of emotional and intellectual development produced a focused, energetic, above-average achiever with great aspirations and artistic talent, but within whom festered a demon of hate that had crept in at age eight. God taught me that I had not only to forgive the School Principal, but also to forgive the moment it all happened. Such forgiveness would take years of divine dealing, for I had feasted on a steady diet of literature by Rap Brown, Angela Davis, Eldridge Cleaver, Nikki Giovanni, Huey Newton, and the brilliant but macabre Richard Wright. Through these and other readings, I had developed a militant mindset and an arrogant distaste for white people.

My mind was in total blackness. These were the tiny black grains of darkness that shot from my head during my first encounter with God. That night God gave me my most important lesson in deliverance: personal deliverance. God later taught me that no matter how many devils are cast out of an individual or how many cases yield the banner of success, by all means make sure that you get your own deliverance.

Chapter 2

THE TERMINATED HONEYMOON

For the next three weeks I arose at six o'clock each morning with uplifted arms and a mouth filled with praise. A life time late sleeper, I routinely arose close to noon. Getting through high school was rough and now in college, I took as many late classes as possible. Breakfast ended at 10:45 a.m., and I was forever barging my way into the Commons, just as the door locked.

Against cafeteria policy, the workers would slip me a bagel and fruit before the food was put away. But now, I was the first one through the Commons door after our prayer session. With face aglow, dramatically changed, the cafeteria crew was awed by me. I remained uncharacteristically mute, but quick to listen to my new spiritual family as they expounded on the Bible. Racing back to my room, I'd examine what had been said by finding it in the scriptures.

Loving all people was as easy as icing a cake. I felt absolutely no pain anywhere and life was like floating on clouds. I awoke each morning to worship and rushed off to a new adventure of discovering God. I saw God in the California sun, in the luscious palm trees, in the ants building a bridge with their own bodies in the Student Court. The flowers took on a whole new beauty and life itself contained an intoxicating fragrance that kept me as high as the stratosphere. Everyone who knew me, knew that I'd been changed. I was marked with the mark of God and did little to hide it.

By the second week, my tongue had been loosed and I began to speak as boldly for Christ as I had for the archenemy of our souls. I spoke of God's redeeming power with a passion that astounded the members of BASIC. Lives were being transformed and God sent me on a soul-winning blitz. Souls were added to the kingdom regularly, as our daily six o'clock prayer band gained momentum and members.

When my girlfriend, Carolyn, came by to see me, I sat her down and told her I was saved. She burst into laughter, until she saw the seriousness on my face. Then she began to cry. We had dated for two years and whatever fun we had was now history. God was asking me to give Him first place. I had no problems with this, for nothing could compare with His love. So sweet was our relationship that I thought that I could never want to be with anyone else again, ever.

Carolyn replied that I was the second boyfriend that she had lost to Christ since being at UCI. The other guy backslid soon after arriving at college, but had been reclaimed by God midstream in their relationship. He led her to the Lord and she, too, experienced the peace of God that passes understanding, but she fell away soon after. I knew that it was not my place to try to restore her, it was my place to say goodbye and end the relationship.

I suddenly jumped up from a deep sleep. Huh? What happened, Lord? It was 8:00 a.m. I was two hours off schedule. I'd awaken at six o' clock sharp for three consecutive weeks without the use of an alarm clock. Those waking moments with Him were glorious ones but now I felt a heaviness in my lower torso. *Oh no,* I thought, *lust is back!* I presumed that God had wiped it completely away. Much to my chagrin, He hadn't. That morning was just the beginning to my dip into the pool of suffering.

Summoned to a surprise suite meeting, members of the dorm expressed their concern about my witness as a new believer. They felt that I was too pushy, forcing others to hear my testimony. I was floored. Not a word was true; however, I received their correction clearly realizing that it was the enemy trying to cool me off.

The next storm occurred during the planning of our BASIC banquet. This year-end extravaganza brought family members, pastors, churches and choirs from as far as Los Angeles. Attendance swelled well over a hundred and I had been unanimously chosen as the Master of Ceremonies by the men, which upset the women of BASIC.

After three banquets moderated by a male, this was their year to have a woman up front. Heated meetings were held behind my back (no one wanted me to be discouraged as a new convert) and finally Gerald called everyone to a prayer meeting. God would make known His choice. By the time I arrived someone said, "The Lord has spoken." The program was to go on as planned. Just how they heard, I did not know, but being a center of controversy made me uncomfortable. Little did I know that this was a precursor to my ministry.

Weeks after the banquet, I received another test. Leon, a gifted Chicano art major in my dorm, came knocking at my door around seven o'clock in the evening. He said, "Come . . . I'll show you . . . come," and took off running. I remembered that before my conversion, Leon had informed me that he had been astral projecting. This dangerous eastern religious practice involves meditating until the outline of the human soul leaves the body and travels within the atmosphere before returning. I had studied the eastern art of meditation and yoga in high school and was intrigued by various principles of Hinduism, and consequently found his experience rather interesting.

Leon had projected twice before, and I half-heartedly suggested that he come get me the next time he did it. This was it. Leon raced across the campus with me in hot pursuit. He ran toward the Science Building, stopped abruptly, pivoted, then headed toward the Humanities Building. Again, he stopped and pointed toward another building. Exhausted, I grabbed him after nearly an hour of this wandering. Leon's roommate joined us and together we sandwiched Leon and slowly headed back to the dormitory.

Leon looked dazed and desperately confused. As he spoke of trying to find his soul and muttered incoherent sentences about truth, something strange manifested and contorted every muscle in his face. In a husky voice and with bulging eyes, he looked squarely at me and said, "You know the truth." I was shocked. This was not Leon's voice I was hearing.

After returning to the dorm we talked with him and I led him to Christ. The next morning with a Bible in hand, Leon followed me to our six o'clock prayer band. "It's beautiful," he muttered softly. The eight kneeling men exploded with praise as I introduced Leon as a new brother in the Lord. Leon was a bit dazed and listless, but I assumed that it was the euphoria one feels when encountering God.

Later that day, Jack said that he had smelled a foul odor coming from Leon as we prayed. He said that it was not a natural body odor, but a scent that eminated from the spirit realm. I didn't have the foggiest idea of what Jack meant but later I learned that Jack was operating in the gift of discerning spirits. I remained speechless and deeply concerned for Leon.

That evening Leon's roommate came knocking on my door to tell that Leon had been acting strangely all day and now he was walking around stark naked. I ran to his darkened room and sure enough, he was unclad, listlessly opening and shutting drawers, in a robotic state. I grabbed him and gently insisted that he put some clothes on. He complied almost like an innocent child would, and we prayed before I left his room. Leon's suite mates camped outside with sleeping bags in front of his door to make sure that he wouldn't wander off during the night. I spent most of the night praying for Leon.

Sometime the following evening his roommate came and got me out of a dance rehearsal. They had rushed Leon to the hospital! He had simply flipped out. As I walked into the dormitory, all eyes were set accusingly on me, the religious fanatic. After a quick shower and change of clothing, four of us sang praises as we drove to the hospital, where the corridor was lined with students. Hours passed before the doctor appeared, but he forbade me to see Leon, stating that only family was permitted visitations at this point.

"I must see him," I said.

"Why?' he asked.

"So that I can pray."

"Prayer, what good can that do?" he said sarcastically.

"In the name of Jesus," I cried, and as sharply as he had refused, he acquiesced and permitted me to see Leon. As I rushed to his bedside I marveled at the power in the name of Jesus. His mother was at his bedside weeping, while stroking his thick brown hair, and asking what had we done to her son. Leon lay on the bed, gaunt, disheveled, and staring blankly into space like a zombie. I was shattered. I comforted his mother and prayed. I heard something within my spirit say that he would come around at 2:00 a.m.

It was nearly midnight when we returned to the dormitory. The lounge was lined with somber students in robes and pajamas, patiently waiting for some answers. Everyone was concerned because everyone loved Leon. As I looked at them watching me, I felt a powerful unction to preach even in the face of the persecuting stares.

"Throw away your Ouija boards . . . burn your astrology books . . . get rid of all this witchcraft . . . Leon is in the hands of God now," I proclaimed.

Sheer pandemonium broke out. Girls went screaming to their rooms, slamming their doors behind them. Those who remained in the lounge knelt, wept and prayed aloud. Repentance was going on throughout the dormitory. A vigil was held most of the night for Leon, and I went to my room weighed down as though the entire world rested on my shoulders.

I did not understand the events that had so drastically changed my fairy-tale walk with the Lord. What I did realize was that the honeymoon was over. God had weaned me from His breastbone and set me in the midst of the valley of Hinnom (fire). There I met the devil face to face through Leon. There I experienced volcanic persecution for the first time for His name's sake; there I tasted the bitter dregs of rejection, false accusation, conspiracy, and misunderstanding.

I would learn later that these elements are just as much of the Christian walk as the joy, peace, and love that we so bountifully feel. They are the essential ingredients that mature us, sober us, equip us for warfare. I had to believe by faith that God loved me no less as I embarked upon these difficult times and that God's purpose for my life would emerge to His glory and honor.

At 2:00 a.m. that morning Leon awakened from his catatonic state. A week later, he was released from the hospital and eventually came back to campus, but he was a different man. Distant and detached, Leon eventually shared the events that led to that dreaded night. According to him, he had soul projected but couldn't find his way back to his body. His first two projections were within the parameter of the dormitory. But the night he knocked on my door was different.

After he projected, another spirit inhabited his body. His soul could not return and it began to soar aimlessly around the campus. When he came to my door, he was asking for my help, while being fully aware that another spirit inhabited him. It was that spirit which spoke through him as we walked back to the dormitory.

When he received prayer in the hospital, his soul was about to return, but this time Christ blocked the reunion and told him many things which he could not divulge. I was dumbfounded. I could neither confirm nor deny what he said. I only knew that dabbling in the occult was as dangerous in the spirit realm as dancing in a den of rattlesnakes is in the natural realm. Little did I know that this mystifying encounter had purpose: God was preparing me for a deliverance ministry.

Chapter 3

GOING HOME

    We sat on the sandy Laguna beach clustered around a camp fire, failing miserably at our attempt to fake joy. This was the last fellowship for BASIC. Exams were behind us, graduation ceremonies lay ahead, and students had already begun the arduous task of packing their belongings for that long trip home. We sang our favorite Christian songs with lumps in our throats and strains of pain in our voices. For me, it was the most dreaded day of my life in Christ. I was about to leave my brothers and sisters without the slightest clue as to when I would see them again. My love for them had abounded to the point of near idol worship, for they had revealed Christ to me. I had thoughts of being with them forever, but this was the fantasy of a babe. God obviously had other plans—returning home to Canton, Ohio was foremost.
    I approached the prospect of returning to Canton with mixed emotions. Canton was a small, family oriented, industrial city where one could quit Timken Roller Bearing in the morning and be hired at Republic Steel the same afternoon. However great that may sound, I didn't want a factory job, nor did I want to get stuck in a small town. Reading books had opened up the world to me as a child, a world that I wanted to see for myself through the vehicle of the performing arts. But now, God was calling me to go home

with a degree in Drama and Dance. I wept most of the night after returning from the beach. Self pity and a fear of what lay ahead in Canton made sleep a torture, but above all, I knew I was going to miss my spiritual family at UCI desperately. When I awoke, I was comforted by the fact that God had seen me through it all. I had gotten my degree in the face of some fierce setbacks.

Unlike the high school ceremonies in Ohio, graduation was held outside in the bright California sun. James, my older and only brother, called to inform me of his plans to fly out for graduation, but I told him not to bother. The ceremony involved a mere transference of a tassel. No names would be called.

On my way to the ceremonies, draped in my cap and gown and seemingly walking on air, I ran into the Dean of Admissions. "Toni Pugh, you made it. Congratulations!" he exclaimed with a broad smile, vigorously shaking my hand. "I never thought I'd see the day! Can I use your name as an example to other students?" I agreed, but had little to say for I knew it was not by my own might or power that I had survived. It was Christ. My purpose for coming to California had been fulfilled. God had opened a door that no man could shut, a door which held my destiny.

Graduating from UCI took sheer perseverance, something I had learned from a race that was held during my sophomore year at Wesleyan. It was a race with a message that revolutionized my life.

During that year, the BSU (Black Student Union) decided to enter the school's annual Greek festival. Traditionally ignored by black students because of a lack of cultural relevance, this year the men registered in the four-man relay race. As the word spread that blacks had entered, the race became a race between the races. As I had said, the black campus population was sparse and isolated from the rest of the University at Wesleyan. When you are in a minority, it is difficult to distinguish between being rejected and putting up a defense of self rejection. Racism builds up such an ugly paranoia, that it's hard to figure out which is occurring. As word circulated, it became the talk of the campus. The white fraternities were determined to win, and of course, we had our eyes set on the same goal.

Five of us practiced daily: passing the baton, running, gauging our starts and getting into condition for the special event. As we timed one another, I had the fastest takeoff, but Al, my roommate, was the overall fastest runner, so I was chosen as the starter and Al was the anchor. The second runner was Michael, Troy was third, and Greg stood in as a backup. The team was impressive, and even though this tiny campus of four thousand stood fragmented by its various fraternities and sororities, the whole school bubbled with excitement over this single event.

As the day approached, the relay became more intense. The black women sparkled with pride and we practiced as though we were running in the Olympics. Things were looking great, until the day of the race. Al pulled a hamstring and couldn't run. Panic hit us like a tidal wave hits an unsuspecting shoreline. The event was less than four hours away. The campus, including the faculty, was seething with anticipation. Greg had to fill in for Al but just as we were regrouping, Troy, fearing a humiliating defeat, quit the team one hour before the race.

The stadium had already begun to fill. It was too late to pull out. We had to find a quick substitute, but no one wanted to enter a race that was due to begin in just a half hour. We finally found an English major named Bruce, who was a chain smoker of non-filtered Camel cigarettes. Without warm up or practice, Bruce gallantly slipped on Al's clothes and got into position on the race track. Michael was set as the first runner and I had become the anchor.

Pure adrenalin flowed through our veins as the official gave us the rules. Before trotting to my position on the other side of the track, I glanced at the black women huddled tightly in the bleachers, ready to cheer their men on. We had never had this kind of unity before. By the time the official raised the gun, the stadium was buzzing with cheers. The gun went off and Michael shot out like a cork from a shaken champagne bottle, and put us in a considerable lead.

The baton was passed to Greg and despite a rough hand off, we maintained our lead. My feet danced nervously as Greg raced around the bend, heading toward Bruce. As Greg raced closer, Bruce anxiously darted toward him ending in a slight collision. The hand off was fumbled. Bruce quickly recovered it but ran out of his lane.

The official blew a whistle and shouted, "BSU is disqualified!" Bruce stopped dead in his tracks. "Keep coming, keep running," I shouted at the top of my voice as the other runners breezed by. When Bruce finally gave me the baton, the other runners were out of sight. I took off running with my heart pumping like a jack hammer. The dimly-lit race track showed no one in sight but I knew that I could catch up if only I ran with all my might. Perhaps I could be a cheetah, or gazelle. I felt confident that we were destined to win the race.

As I went around the bend, I put on more speed. I thought about the victory of Jesse Owens at the 1936 Olympics when Hitler was touting the superiority of his Aryan athletes. I thought about Jackie Robinson grand slamming in the major leagues amid the angry protest of bigoted fans. I thought of the inspiring depiction in Maya Angelou's "I Know Why the Caged Bird Sings;" of Joe Louis winning the heavy weight championship against Carnera, proving that "we were the strongest people in the world."[1] These flashing thoughts gave me strength and the assurance that I could catch up and win. After all, it was nothing new for us to be the underdog but emerge as victors. My momentum increased.

With squinting eyes and a heaving chest, I completed the bend with beads of perspiration rolling off my face. As I approached the final stretch, I could see no other runners. What I did see were chariots and girls dressed in tunics preparing for the next event. I increased my speed. As I zoomed across the finish line gasping for air and bent over with exhaustion, the devastating reality hit. We had come in dead last.

Someone approached me but to this day I couldn't tell you who it was. I was nearly blinded by perspiration and tortured by an indescribable hurt. Grasping frantically for air, I pushed them away and searched for my clothes. I tried to block out all sight and sound, wishing that I were an eagle. I would fly away to the mountains and be at rest and never return to the civilized world. I wanted to run out of the stadium to my dormitory but exhaustion overcame me. I was simply numb. Better that a man never existed than to suffer the pain I felt throbbing in my bones.

Somehow I managed to get to my room with Bruce following soon after. We both stood there, glassy eyed, voices racked with pain, afraid to release our emotions in front of one another. Bruce tried to apologize, but I stopped him. It wasn't his fault. He was a real hero to step in at the last minute. It was no one's fault. I choked and turned away, until he changed clothes and left the room. It was not a moment too soon. I fell to the bed, buried my face into my pillow and howled like a wounded dog before falling asleep inside a pool of humiliation.

It was days before I could show my face in public. When I did go to the cafeteria for lunch, a young lady named Jamille caught me and gave me a huge hug with her sturdy, mahogany arms.

"You did it," she said excitedly. "We're so proud of you, Toni!"

"But Jamille, we lost the race," I said sadly.

"When we didn't see you coming around the bend with the rest of the runners, we assumed that something had happened on the other side of the track. Michael gave us such a lead. When the other runners came around the bend and crossed the finish line our hopes were dashed. We were shell-shocked. Everyone was looking at each other, asking what happened to the team. Then you came streaking out of the darkness like lightning! We started screaming and jumping and when you crossed the finish line, all the ladies started chanting, our mighty black men, our mighty black men, our mighty black men! Didn't you hear us?"

"But, Jamille," I reiterated, "we lost."

It was then that Jamille spoke with the wisdom of an angel.

"That's not the point, Toni. The point is that you finished the race. You see, anybody can start something, but it takes a real man to finish what he has started. All the ladies are so proud of you, Toni."

I stood in a daze. The words Jamille spoke surpassed any knowledge I had acquired at Wesleyan, a university ranked among the top schools in the country. These words would help me survive

Irvine; would aid me in my walk with the Lord; would sustain me through thirteen rigorous years in the pastorate; must echo in the ear drums of humanity for generations to come . . . "don't worry about where you place, just finish the race."

With the graduation ceremony concluded, I was back to the dorm for the last time. Packing was quite a chore. Every square inch of each bag was filled to capacity. Herb was on his way to take me to the bus station to ship my bags, then I would meet Gerald who would take me to the airport. As I scanned the empty apartment for the last time, my eyes fell upon a stack of albums strung neatly and lying against the living room wall. I had forgotten to pack my albums.

I had collected some real gems over the years at UCI, a mixture of rhythm and blues, jazz, some classic dance music, and plenty of Aretha. As I pondered what to do, it came to my mind simply to leave them. Listening to that type of music was history. God was calling me to sacrifice my Isaac upon Mount Moriah, for I loved both music and dance. This call to lay aside something dear would be a mere whisper of the things God would ask me to forsake in the years to come.

Leon stopped by before leaving the campus for summer break. He intended to return next fall and finish his degree in art. We embraced like two long lost brothers reuniting for the first time. "God sent you here," he whispered. With that, he left me with the saddest gaze in my eyes. Leon was still not who he once was.

It was off to the bus station, but not before Herb and I knelt down to pray the sinners' prayer. Herb was ready to surrender to Christ and became another brother born into the family of God on UCI. The BASIC fellowship was growing steadily. From the time that I was saved in March until graduation, God was giving us a new convert each week. This was due to the daily prayer band and witnessing that had been established. God was teaching BASIC the power and the importance of prayer. It allows us to accomplish in the spirit realm that which cannot be done through natural strength. It humbles the soul.

We were air-borne within minutes. After refreshments were served, my mind drifted back to Irvine. God had done a marvelous work in me and had used my testimony to stir many. Besides the incident with Leon, I had begun to see through that thin veil that separates the natural realm from the spiritual. One incident that stood out was the day I was witnessing to Hank.

Hank was an affable, down-to-earth brother who possessed a remarkable balance of intellectual, athletic and leadership prowess. A pre-med major, destined to be a second generation doctor, we became Resident Assistants the same year and both reapplied for the position the following year. I was selected again but Hank wasn't. Housing became an issue for Hank, so I let him stay at my place whenever he needed to. I remember an encounter with racism in Costa Mesa left me with my bags out in the streets. I ended up back in the dormitory study lounge unable to attend classes that had already began. God saw me through it all, and my doors were opened to homeless strangers ever since. I couldn't let anyone go through the things I had encountered in California if I could help it.

One day Hank and I stood in the quad talking about Christ. The conversation was intense and in a near debate mode when we simultaneously saw Trudy walk across the quad. As I continued witnessing, our eyes remained fastened upon Trudy, not merely because she was an exceptional beauty, but because the Holy Spirit wanted to show us both something. In an instant, Trudy's head turned sharply, her countenance twisted, and she veered toward us with a frown. When she approached, her frown softened to a seductive smile.

"What are you two handsome men talking about?"

There was a flirtatious giggle and then an abrupt goodbye but not before she planted a kiss upon my lips. I was astonished. Trudy was one of the nicest girls on campus; an unpretentious beauty. This simply was not her behavior.

As she walked away, Hank said, "I know what you are going to say, Pugh."

"Right," I affirmed. "That was the devil. He didn't want me to talk to you about Christ." Hank responded in disbelief and whatever work the Holy Spirit was doing had broken. I also recalled the day Hank came to my room and said that he'd give me six months, then said with eyes squinting, "I'll give you a year, Pugh," before I would be back to my "old" self. He later confided that when he heard the news of my conversion, he fell on his bed and cried because he knew that I would throw my life away like so many professing Christians he had known. The Holy Spirit shielded my heart from these wounding words and assured me that Hank's tears were over Him and not me.

My retrospective daydream was interrupted by the flight attendant gathering up my unfinished snack. I sighed. Spirits do indeed exist and they do influence people—even good people. I had applied to and was later rejected from a Master's program in creative writing at the University of Iowa. Little did I realize that God was preparing to give me an associate degree in demonology.

Chapter 4

DEEPER LIFE

Returning home wasn't as bad as I had imagined. Mom was her usual warm, jovial self, showing the signs of age but ever so gracefully. My brother and older sister, James and Bettie, were both unsaved and shocked at my new lifestyle, especially James. Being several years older than I, he had taken pleasure in giving his little brother the keys to his Cadillac and apartment for entertainment purposes. But those days were long gone. I was a new creature in Christ Jesus. My passion was no longer for the fleeting pleasures that night life offered, but for Christ and Him alone. God had assured me that they, too, would follow my example and they did. Within eight weeks of my arrival, my brother and sister were sweetly saved by the blood of the Lamb. God granted me the awesome privilege of leading them both to Him.

My running buddies were clearly turned off at my testimony. One childhood friend, Chris, stopped by with some harsh words of criticism. He spoke about how my conversion had put a breach in our childhood friendships. Moments before he arrived, God had warned me that someone was coming with a challenge and to treat them with love. I did just that, and within weeks, Chris was born again and on fire for God. He went to Washington, D.C., got his girlfriend Cheryl saved, married her and moved her back to Canton all within months. God was moving in a mighty way.

I maintained a steady diet of the Word of God which I devoured with such a voracity that it would be accurate to say that I was a fanatic, but hardly in the negative sense of the word. I was deeply devoted to Him; addicted to His presence, carried away by the power of His Words, expressly in love with Him in the most inexplicable way. Only God could understand my affection for Him—for in Him I found my heart's longing: the epitome of Truth, the essence of Love, the sincerity of Friendship. I could not resist loving Him. Everyone who had known me previously could recognize it.

My first objective was to find gainful employment, but God wanted to get me planted into a church. While returning from a job interview downtown, I ran into a dear friend who shared that she had just gotten saved under a new ministry in town at the YWCA, only weeks before. We rejoiced and embraced as I shared that I, too, was a new convert. The founder's name was Hezekiah Farrell.

I arrived at the Tuesday night Bible study held upstairs and sat amid some seventy unfamiliar faces. The preacher was a tall, dark, distinguished-looking West Indian from the island of Montserrat. By the age of thirty he had pioneered seven churches, five in the islands, and two in the United States, and had an evangelical outreach in London, England.

He proclaimed that God had sent him to Canton to build a church and to raise up an army of disciples. After an hour of Bible teaching, his claim was irrefutable. He turned Revelations into a living reality under what I later learned was the anointing of the Holy Ghost.

Upon closing, something I had never seen before occurred. He walked down the aisles laying hands on various ones who subsequently fell to the ground. The melodious piano music played by a woman named Sister Johnson, failed to set a graceful tone to the sound of metal chairs sliding across the floor and banging shut.

As some began to speak in an indiscernible language, others began to shout, while others, mostly women, fell lifelessly to the floor. I was speechless.

What disturbed me most was the scene I saw up front. A lady lay unconscious on the floor with her mouth open and out of it flowed a copious stream of saliva. Another woman knelt prayerfully beside her with paper towels absorbing what looked like bubbling suds. She softly uttered the name, "Jesus." There was more yelling, more falling, more people speaking in a strange, mysterious language. Very little frightened me in life but this scene had cracked my bravado. I grabbed my Bible and scurried out of the room. Just as I crossed the threshold, I heard the voice of God speaking to my spirit, "Don't be afraid . . . this is the church I have chosen to raise you up in." I was enshrouded by a calm, but I had seen enough and darted out of the building.

The following few days I was led to Berean Christian Bookstore in town and there, as I browsed various books filed under the Charismatic section, God explained the move of the Holy Spirit. Sometime later I was given a book entitled, *Pigs in the Parlor* written by Frank and Ida Mae Hammond. It was a brilliant exposition and revelation on the deliverance ministry, perhaps the most insightful in publication to this day.

A week later, I was filled with the Holy Ghost and spoke with other tongues. My devotion to Christ was magnified a hundredfold. I would spend perpetual hours in the Word, taking breaks only for sleep and meals. I trod a straight path from church to home until I found a job working at the Red Lobster. God was doing a deep work in me. However deeply I loved Him, much had to be surrendered to God: ambitions, greed, pride, anger, rebellion, unforgiveness, retaliation, lust, selfish plotting and an endless list of fleshly areas that are being dealt with to this very day.

The work of God upon the human soul is monumental. The Potter's loving hands mold and shape until the vessel is honorable in His sight. The flame of the fire is excruciating but necessary for the final display. Impurities must be burned out. Thinking must be renewed. His name is to be given the praise through the godly works of His transformed vessels. I was so honored to be chosen to do the works that were laid down before the foundation of the earth. I was so captivated by His love that I could only surrender to this process of sanctification.

During this time of consecration I experienced something that made my encounter with Leon look like a sitcom. A dear sister and I were visiting an inmate in the Stark County Jail. While in the parking lot I saw a tall guy, whom I knew from childhood, walking twenty feet ahead of us. My spirit quivered because I saw something strangely evil about his eyes. I believe it was a demon manifestation.

As we stood in the crowded lobby, I saw him turn and stare at me. I suddenly lost my balance and released a shrieking cry while grabbing hold of a vending machine to keep from falling. I felt as though I was chained to a roller coaster bound for the outer limits. My heart pounded as my strength abated, and I knew I had to leave the area immediately.

That summer of the following year, I had caught the bus to Cardinal Wilson, a store in a small plaza on the Southwest end of town. Having gotten a bag full of groceries, I decided to take a stroll while awaiting the bus. As I peered through the windows of several shops, my eye caught a glimpse of the same guy I had seen at the jailhouse. Even though he didn't see me, I suddenly felt like I was on the roller coaster again, but this time it was taking a violent plunge downward. I cried out and ran as the bus pulled up and whisked me home.

I barely had enough strength to carry the bag into the house. I fell on the couch and there I lay helplessly bound, without strength to even move. I silently pleaded with God to help me because I couldn't utter a word. Nothing could describe the way I felt, except that on one hand, I had a burning hatred for God; on the other hand, there was a silent, but real love for Him. I was trapped within this nightmarish chasm, unable to move. I prayed myself out of this catatonic state and called a friend for some answers.

"It was witchcraft. It was draining your very life from you. In fact, you didn't have any life, except what came from the Holy Ghost" she said emphatically. After praying for me she said, "You're marked. The witches in Canton know that God has a great work for you to do."

About a week after I was fully recovered, Chris came by with a very perplexed look on his face.

"Toni, I had a dream about you, but it was so bad and I didn't really want to tell you," he said.

The dream consisted of a stadium filled with cheering fans. Two teams were on the field; one was quite huge, like giants, and the other was regular size. I was on the latter of the two teams and whatever the game was (something very similar to football), I was quite gifted. Whenever I carried the ball, touchdowns were made and it would send the crowd into a frenzy. Suddenly the opposing team was in a huddle, clearly plotting against me.

"During the next play, one of these men grabbed you by your face mask, picked you up and slammed you to the ground, Toni. You were seriously hurt, because stars were floating around you. I said, oh no!"

The dream ended when I began ascending upward and Chris started searching for me. I received a powerful witness in my spirit. I told him that he was a bit late. The attack had already occurred.

The interpretation of the dream was made clear at church that night. The ball represented the Word of God. The giants, a type of Goliath and his brothers, represented the ruling spirit over Canton, which is witchcraft. I had received a power drainage. Little else was revealed and believe me, I didn't want to know any more. I was awestricken. I had no idea that this could happen in Christianity, besides, I never bothered anyone. My paths were straight: home, work, and then church. Just why this was happening to me was baffling. I prayed all the more.

As I grew in grace and the knowledge of God, I realized just how great the anointing at Deeper Life was, and just what God was offering through the ministry: a deeper life in Him. The church was full of the power and the Word of God, and had an international outreach. I was flowing in the life of the Spirit of God, water baptized and made a deacon in the church within a few months. After six months of working at Red Lobster, I took my savings and traveled to the islands of Antigua and Barbuda on my first missionary trip with Dr. Farrell and fellow ministers.

During my foreign trip, I met and bonded with a brother with a towering figure and a basso voice named Carlos from London, England. God taught me many things through Carlos, especially concerning manhood. I remember coming into the all-brick Antiguan parish and Carlos asking me where my dirty clothes were. I showed him and he quickly snatched them up, underwear and all, and began hand washing them in spite of my protest. After the wash was dry, Carlos pressed every piece of outward clothing. I was taken aback. "Brother, I would never do this for you. Besides this is considered women's work," I said sadly.

He held up his huge hand as to silence me and replied, "However I would treat Jesus is how I will treat you."

My heart melted. God was adjusting me with His blowtorch of love. He was giving me another look at manhood.

Carlos and I grew closer each day, much like David and Jonathan. I felt that God had given me a lifelong friend in the gospel. We spent literal hours in the Bible, discussing, laughing, debating, praising, and weeping. Outside of Dr. Farrell, I had never met a man so intensely Biblical as he. His down-to-earth interpretation, coupled with a wry sense of humor, made me hold him in high esteem. He admired my youthful, fiery zeal, and together we felt that we could evangelize the world. Departing was tough; beautiful people are always infectious. We vowed never to allow distance and time to separate our friendship. If God would say the same, we determined to see one another again. Until then, letters would have to suffice.

The following year, after getting a job at our electric company as a data processor, God granted us our vow. I traveled to London, England, for two weeks with Dr. Farrell and our church organist, Sister Helen Johnson. I resided with Carlos and his lovely wife, Dora, and their two adorable boys. I stayed at home while the boys were in school and Carlos and Dora worked days. During this time I spent most of my time in prayer and Bible study and then it was off to the evening Crusades. The West Indian people are some of the hardest-working people on the planet. Fervent in worship, steadfast in their dedication, entrenched in family values; I was hooked on the culture.

Dora came home from an eight-hour factory job, prepared a full course meal, did dishes, bathed the boys, and prepared for the next morning like clockwork. During the week she'd soak the clothes, including mine, then haul them to the laundromat for washing. She'd press them as well as any American dry cleaning service, then clean the house, and repeat the routine.

Dinner was prepared each evening in lavish style: curry goat, rice and pigeon peas, fresh bread and plenty of curry gravy, a side dish of vegetables and a cool Carribean punch. As a non-cooking bachelor, I thought I was in heaven. Just watching her work without complaint or drudgery was exhausting. I felt a bit guilty especially when Dora and Carlos gave me their master bedroom and slept in separate beds in the boys' room my entire stay. I protested but they insisted. This was a cultural gesture. I assured them that it wouldn't be like that in America and they laughed. Again God was teaching me, this time it was about the gift of hospitality.

While Carlos and Dora worked, I was being whisked around London by an energetic young tour guide named Holly. Holly was not only a great conversationalist but also exceptionally pleasant. I'll never forget the morning when she suddenly swooped up something from the ground and stuffed it in my hand while we walked down a busy London street. After a block, I opened my hand to find a wad of several pounds someone had obviously lost. We howled with laughter and praised God as we went to the nearest fish and chips shop.

When it was time to depart, Holly, Carlos and another sister accompanied us to the airport. Just as boarding was announced, Holly grabbed me by the arm, pulled me aside and with a smack dead on the lips, said, "if it is the Lord's will." Through calls and letters, Holly made her romantic interest known. I was rather neutral to it all because I was in love with Jesus.

Later that year, Holly flew into Canton for a week and stayed at Sister Johnson's home. I took vacation time to show her the town being cautious not to give the wrong impression. While at the Monument Park, Holly confessed that she had fallen in love with me from the very first. She had told God that the situation was breaking her heart so she had come to Canton to get a confirmation that I was the man for her. If I wasn't, she wanted a release from me altogether. I admired her honesty and strength of character but I was only mildly interested.

I couldn't rule out the possibility, so we attended some local meetings in Massillon, featuring guest speakers and prophets, John and Paula Sandford. I had read two excellent books by them, "*The Elijah Task* and *Transformation of the Inner Man.*" We attended several services in hope that God would provide clarity, but we heard nothing. The Sanfords dealt with some issues concerning forgiveness that hit home, however.

During a very tender moment Holly shared that she had been born out of wedlock. At the age of four she could vividly recall the day that her father abandoned them, leaving her mother shattered over the rejection. Bitter hatred toward men of similar status crept in at that point. We prayed for that little girl to be healed and ended the evening with dinner.

An early flight out of Akron-Canton afforded little time but to greet Sister Johnson then pray. As we did, Holly suddenly cracked and screamed in agony. Falling upon me and then to the floor she wept uncontrollably. She lay on the carpet shaking and groaning as if she was having convulsions.

"My heart, God, I cannot stand it, my heart . . . my heart."

With eyes swollen with tears, I looked helplessly at Sister Johnson. I picked Holly up from the floor and laid her on the couch. She was still moaning and shrieking.

"I cannot stand it, God . . . my heart . . . God," she howled.

"God bless you, Toni," said Sister Johnson softly as I departed.

When I got into the car, I drove down Route 62 like a madman. I cried uncontrollably. I had suffered so dearly in my walk with God and now I had caused Holly to suffer too. I felt like I was under a curse of some sort. It was only God's grace that got me home that night.

The next morning I called to tell Holly that I was on my way to get her.

"I'm not going!" she said.

"What?"

"I canceled the flight. I've got to get this thing settled, once and for all."

I sighed in disbelief. We spent the next two days going in rounds like two boxers.

"Holly, did I ever do anything to make you feel this way about me while in England?"

"No," she said.

"What about since you've been here in Canton?"

"You've been a perfect gentleman," she replied.

"Then what on earth is happening?"

"All I know is that I can't get you out of my spirit. It's tormenting. I've prayed and prayed but you won't go away. I've asked the Lord to release me many times but you are still there."

"You know that I don't feel that same way about you, don't you?" I added, slowly.

"I know. This is an issue between the Lord and me," she said tearfully.

I regretted ever opening my mouth. I did not want to cause her any more pain. Yet, I had to set the record straight. I had done nothing to stir these emotions; therefore, I could not be held accountable. Working day shift and dealing with Holly during the evenings, had made life exhausting.

After two days our talking had turned into heated debates. At my insistence, Holly finally booked her flight and left Canton. I stopped by Sister Johnson's home.

"Sister Johnson, I never so much as touched her!" I said.

"I know, Toni," she told me. "We were up all night. This girl is in love, Toni, I mean really in love. Phew! You could write a book!"

On my list of foreign travel came Jamaica. Dr. Farrell, accompanied by Sister Johnson, held dynamic meetings in Kingston and Mandeville. When I arrived at the tent meeting, Dr. Farrell was thrashing the hosts of hell as he preached.

While scanning the audience my eyes fell upon a familiar face. It was Holly. She was visiting relatives when she heard about the Crusade. Together, we spent two delightful weeks canvassing the beautiful island. Holly's wit, charm, faith, and inner strength were unfailing. Spiritually, she was in tune with God and by the end of my stay I must admit that I had grown fond of her.

Back in Canton, God was doing an awesome undercover work raising up the fivefold ministry gifts. You could literally ask God a question Saturday night in prayer and hear the answer Sunday morning across the pulpit. The anointing was so heavy that many times we had to literally carry the women out of the hall to their cars. God was doing so great a work that it amazed everyone. I stayed under the power of God continuously, sometimes falling to the floor before I could make the altar call.

After church, I retained my insatiable thirst for God which overrode my desire for food. I often fasted: five days and five nights, twenty-one days and nights, one day a week for a year, and spontaneous weekend fasts. I had to put a safety pin in my pants to hold them up. Eating was never important to me especially being in the performing arts. Even at banquets you had to eat like a mouse because performance required it.

Not long after coming to Canton I received what I thought a direct command from the Lord. "*I am the Almighty God; walk before me, and be thou perfect*" (Genesis 17:1). I did not hear a voice, but felt a strong impression in my spirit as I studied the life of Abraham. The command was literal. Although I was making decent money working swing shift as a data processor, I couldn't buy a car. God wanted me to walk and so I walked to work, church and home in Ohio's blustering winters and sulking summers for years. I caught the bus when necessary, but basically it was a walk with God.

Every step I took was a death march to the cross. Daily, I was losing my rights in this life. I knew that God would settle for nothing less than a total surrender. He wanted all of my Isaacs. My natural propensity toward being stubborn kicked up a ferocious war, but God won. He always does. He let me know that someone would give me a car when my test was over. I had to die to the thought of having my own until the Father said otherwise. It became a bittersweet suffering.

An entire era of fashion, entertainment, politics, and economic changes had transpired unnoticed by me. I remember going to a family reunion in Tennessee and asking who was on a poster in my teenage cousin's room. "You don't know who Prince is?" she asked in amazement. I was shocked when a coworker told me that money could be drawn out of an ATM from the street side. I was equally amazed when I realized that my platform shoes and bell bottom pants, all that I had in my wardrobe, were no longer fashionable-amazed and disappointed because I thoroughly liked both. I became largely a recluse, preferring solitude, which would prove to be a manifold dilemma in the plans God had for me.

The work God wanted me to do was to succeed Dr. Farrell as pastor. I dreaded the thought because the depth of his spiritual ministry exceeded anything I had ever witnessed live or by television. Besides, there were three associate ministers fully ordained and placed in the pulpit. I was in the pews relatively unrecognized. Also, the enemy had sown tares among the wheat and the ministry rocked with division from evil workers on a continual basis. Our growth was stymied by internal wars.

The ministry was reaching hundreds before I arrived. Dr. Farrell literally shook the city. By the time I joined, the numbers had dwindled to seventy. Among them we had workers of iniquity thrashing everyone in sight, seeking to shut down the work of God through gossip, slander, innuendo, and rebellion. This persisted primarily among the ladies. When Dr. Farrell began his international travel, the anointing faded, membership dwindled, and the work appeared ready to close. All but one associate minister had left. I was the only young man in the congregation and only a small remnant remained. Bound by insecurity and shyness, I had developed a preference for privacy and seclusion. Standing before people was at best, unappealing. So I sat on the church pew knowing His will, but being unwilling to do anything about it.

I was brought into the valley of decision by a married couple, Eon and Henrietta. While returning from an evangelistic service, Henrietta prophesied from Akron to Canton, some twenty miles. God kept asking, "How long would I deny Him . . . how long before I do His will?" This went on until I was dropped off at work.

While working the midnight shift alone, God continued ministering to me. I wept as His power descended upon me like a cool cloud. He reminded me of the years He had protected and kept me from the destroyer and now I could not do this for Him. I broke down weeping and told Him I would do anything but I needed a push to step into the pulpit.

Years of seclusion had opened me up to spirits of shyness, low self esteem, and reluctance. Although I wanted to obey God, such a restraint lay deep within my bosom, I just couldn't go forward. I had become like Peter, James and John who, upon seeing the glory in the mount, wanted to build tabernacles and stay, neglecting the tiresome work of casting out devils awaiting in the valley (Matt. 17).

That very next Sunday night Dr. Farrell preached a powerful message from the Gospel of Matthew, Chapter 25. It dealt with the parable of the talents. His closing remark on the servant who hid one talent was, "*and cast ye the unprofitable servant into outer darkness: there shall be weeping and gnashing of teeth*" (v. 30). Then Dr. Farrell spoke very plainly, "somebody in here has something to tell me tonight."

Three people ran up to the altar that night. Without the slightest idea of what the other two needed, I knew God had spoken to me in no uncertain terms. I was to preach or it would be outer darkness. I had my incentive.

"God wants me to preach!" I said frantically to Dr. Farrell.

"When?" he asked.

"Immediately," I cried.

The date was set for the following Sunday night. I took my text from Luke's Gospel, Chapter 8, concerning the woman with the issue. After I finished preaching, spit was everywhere. Everyone was full of joy and amazement, including Dr. Farrell. Only God and I knew what it took to get me up there. I was relieved that it was over and happy that through obedience God was pleased, and perhaps even had a smile upon His blessed face.

Chapter 5

First Encounter: Jezebel

More sermons and teachings followed, astonishing the small group of followers, including Dr. Farrell. It became apparent that His hand was upon my life. The anointing of God will always distinguish those who are called to do a work. Despite some resistance from the enemy, God's will prevailed and Dr. Farrell called me into his office and asked me what the Lord was speaking to my heart concerning Deeper Life in Canton. This was no time for modesty, no time to beat around the bush. The devil had tried upon several occasions to shut the ministry down completely. Despair had risen to such a height during Dr. Farrell's absences that some Sunday mornings the church did not open simply because no one decided to come. During a severe Ohio winter, Sunday services were abandoned altogether. I told Dr. Farrell that God wanted me to take the church on as the pastor.

Within weeks, the announcement was made, my papers arrived, and an ordination service was held. I never once exalted myself. God had told me years prior to this blessed event that all would be taken care of by Him at the appropriate time. He was right. What is happening today by many well-intending but misguided brothers and sisters who long to be in the pulpit is self exaltation. They cannot wait to be placed into their ministerial posts. They do not realize that He who called them can also place them where He wills.

I had meticulously devoured the story of David and studied how he never sought to seize the throne that was divinely his. Watchmen Nee's book, *Spiritual Authority*, offers the Body of Christ some powerful insight on the subject of kingdom authority. Self-exaltation is not a kingdom principle. It will always lead to abasement. So crucial was this matter, that I later implemented the book in our church Bible study.

I stepped into the pastorate at the same time that Benigno Aquino, President Ferdinand Marcos' chief political opponent, was assassinated in the Philippines. His wife, Corazon Aquino, bravely took the vacant spot as the nation's leader. As the first female president of this volatile country, she was captured by a photographer kneeling childlike at the altar with her face fixed toward the heavens. She was asking for direction. I wept. I desperately needed direction too. My day had arrived but so had the greatest challenge of my life.

When Holly heard of my ordination, she flew in from England for a week, for her second visit to Canton. She was becoming more aggressive in her pursuit, while I remained uncommitted and focused on the pastorate. She felt that I needed a wife now more than ever but I felt that I needed no distractions. Like Nehemiah, it was time to focus on rebuilding the languishing work in Canton.

I took over a church that had only one service a week. Our Tuesday night Bible study had long been abandoned; so had Sunday school, communion, water baptism and prayer. The absence of children made a youth ministry unnecessary. Though we had an expensive Hammond organ, drums, a solid oak baby grand piano, we had no musicians; and naturally the morale of the remnant was decidedly low. I was the only single young man in the church and had been for years.

My first aim was to clean the sanctuary thoroughly. Along with the ladies, Sister Farrell, who stood gallantly beside me, two church mothers, and two deacons, we set out to wash, scrub, polish, paint, vacuum, dust every square inch of the place. My next task was to restore Tuesday night Bible study, morning Sunday school, and open the church for prayer every day at noon. Communion was restored the first Sunday of every month and new song books were ordered. I was preaching and teaching every service and ministered from endless material acquired from my years of consecrated study. The word was getting around that Deeper Life, the Titanic, was afloat and members of long ago, as well as new faces, began to show up and join the fellowship.

I was optimistic that the ministry God had given me could reach masses. Deeper Life had its own brand of uniqueness that went beyond shoreline Christianity. There are four types of fishermen: those who sit on the shore and fish, those who venture out with waist boots, still others who get out in motor boats to fish for the bigger catch, and those who fish way out in the deep in charter boats. Deeper Life was a ministry that launched out into the deep.

We reestablished ties with our sister church in Boston, inviting them down and flying up for mutual meetings and fellowship. This I did while working swing shifts and walking every day to both work and church. I swayed from exhilaration to exhaustion. My love for God and the people was genuine, but my understanding of the pastorate was minuscule. Besides having no formal training for ministry, I was ignorant of the spirit world and the role demons play within the church. But that was about to change. God was ready to open a door into the enemy's camp. There, I would meet my number one nemesis; there I would meet and ultimately defeat the spirit of Jezebel.

What started as a very happy, energetic "college approach" to pastoring soon fizzled into sheer exasperation. I did everything I thought a good leader was supposed to do: bend over backwards, remain mute amid public challenges from disgruntled members and out-of-order testimonies, involve myself in every activity of the church including cleaning and cutting the lawn, visit sick members in the hospital, chase crack addicts and potential suicide victims down the street trying to convince them that both Jesus and I loved them, give away anything I had, refuse an income, and just maintain a cheerful optimism.

Of course this is not the role of a pastor at all, but rather the role of a well-intending man headed for a disaster. I was suffering from what is known as the Messianic complex: you've got to be there for everyone. Needless to say, despite church growth, I was depleted of strength and on the verge of an emotional and physical breakdown.

Despite my best efforts, nothing helped the church to get off the ground. The spiritual bondage among the people was pervasive. The power to reach them exceeded my ability to give. Endless hours of counseling were spent in the homes of single mothers on the brink of mental breakdowns, young ex-cons fresh from prison, families with money management problems, and scores of crack, alcohol and sexual addicts. Although I was full of the Word, compassion, and sincerity; and though I made my love for the people evident, when it was time to paint the pews, mow the lawn, and raise offerings, they were not there. The spiritual climate in Canton was dreadful. My spirit began to evaporate in a heat of exhaustion, disappointment, and hurt.

Besides this, within the church I was receiving some not-so-subtle opposition from one individual who had a teaching post during our Bible study. If I called the congregation to the altar for united prayer, this woman would remain defiantly in her seat while other members would approach hesitantly, looking nervously behind them. After service, they would scurry out into the foyer whispering about me. The spirit of Jezebel was at work.

Historically, Jezebel was a Zionist priestess who married King Ahab during the ministry of the prophets Elijah and Elisha. She controlled the throne, using Ahab as a mere facade. Her name means "unhusbanded or uncovered." The irony is that she possessed both a husband and covering but refused to be under either. She single-handedly turned the hearts of Israel from Jehovah worship to Baal, a Phoenician deity that placed emphasis on sensuality. She intensely hated God's prophets and had killed all His servants except Elijah and those who were hidden away in caves. Ruthless and defiant, her chief aim was to thwart the plans of God, and take control of the religious order by removing the man of God from the scene.

In I Kings, Chapter 19, we see the demise of Jezebel. In II Kings 2, Elijah was transported by chariots into heaven. Both are taken from the earthly scene but the spirit of both exist today. Jesus Himself said, *"Elijah must first come and restore all things. And if ye will receive it this is Elijah, which was for to come"* (Matthew 11:14). John the Baptist caught the mantle of Elijah and operated under the same anointing as Elijah. The spirit of Jezebel was operating through a woman in the church of Thyratira in Revelations, Chapter 2. This proves that though Jezebel and Eliljah are gone, the spirits that motivated both are alive and well. We need the anointing of Elijah desperately, for he brings a much needed revival to the earth (Malachi 4:5–6). But the spirit of Jezebel is a major principality over our nation and must be trodden under foot by spiritual warfare. Unfortunately, many women have unwittingly caught her mantle and are being used mightily to come against the servants of the Lord Jesus Christ.

Exposed

The Jezebel spirit had crept into our midst through an individual who was teaching Bible study at the time. She used her teaching platform for propaganda, subtly casting a negative light upon me and my ministry to the congregation. At first I thought it was a mere friction between us, but later I found it was far more serious than I could ever imagine. Members who loved and respected me dearly began to eye me suspiciously and respond to my leadership with defiance. Initially I ignored it and became self absorbed in proving that I was sincere, honest and had nothing to hide. But the more transparent I became, the worse my relationship with the congregation got. As the opposition to my leadership became more evident, the more angry I grew, until even messages on God's love thundered across the pulpit in furious rebukes. I was falling into the hands of the enemy but knew no other way to fight. Clearly my authority was being undermined. The congregation was uncooperative and resistant because of this one individual who sat reticently by, while her eunuchs did all the protesting, squabbling and complaining. I'd call the congregation together for a general church cleaning and no one would show up. I'd shrug my shoulders and clean the building myself. Anything I instituted was opposed and it was clear that she was planting seeds of discord among the congregation.

The rift between our congregation and me widened when I moved from my mother's house to an apartment only blocks from the church but told no one. My new telephone number was unpublished and I had no intentions of giving it out. My response to Jezebel's wrath was to hide as Elijah did. My cave was my apartment. Many nights I would sit for hours in darkness with only the moonlight diffusing through my window shades. *What on earth are you doing, God?* I thought. I had such hopes for the ministry, such a desire to see the work prosper. No amount of fasting, studying, or consecration was too great and yet it seemed all in vain. I was shattered and felt that I could trust absolutely no one.

At night I would fall into bed too tired to pray, too wounded to care that I hadn't. I drifted between fatalistic resignation and utter despair. "Oh God," I'd cry, "how is it that some men of God can realize their dreams of excellence, success and grandeur while others are faced with the horrifying reality of defeat and yet serve the same God?" Is God biased? Are some called into a life of opulence and worldwide acceptance, while others are called to struggle endlessly under the bitter whip of rejection and obscurity? Should I be angry that I would taste the latter of the two extremes or should I count it all joy that God called me? These and a myriad of other thoughts flashed through my mind like a panorama until I was spun into a comfortless sleep.

Scripturally, God uses men from varied backgrounds for various purposes, all for His glory. Most of the men God used in the Bible were prophets. Abraham, Jacob, David experienced great elevations in the Lord while Moses and Jeremiah ministered in the pits of despair and rejection. What right has the clay to say to the Potter, "What are you doing with my life?" The answer is clear:

First Encounter: Jezebel

none. Yet I wanted to argue with God, to hold a conference with Him, like Job in the 28th chapter.

But alas, He would not be persuaded to change my course, neither would He hear me, I thought. Since I was not a quitter, I simply went through the motions of pastoring while despising every moment of it. I was at a loss at what to do. At first glance I thought I was fighting a deceitful, backstabbing woman in the congregation with a personal vendetta against me but God opened my eyes to see what was going on in the realm of the spirit.

Visions

I received understanding of the situation when God gave me two visions. The first vision opened with a rolling green pasture full of sheep grazing placidly about. I was in the midst of the flock clothed in a shepherd's cloak with a hood that covered my face. As the sheep bleated and grazed, I moved effortlessly about with a long staff in my right hand. Suddenly, I noticed a sheep separated from the rest of the flock. It peered intently toward the herd. This sheep had a beautiful fleece, about twice the size of the others but when I looked closer I noticed blood dripping from its mouth. *Blood*, I thought. *It's impossible. Sheep aren't carnivorous.*

As my eyes looked closely at the mouth of this sheep, it began to snarl, revealing blood stained, yellow fangs. "This is not a sheep. It's a wolf," I concluded. Then a voice spoke in the vision, "Yea, thou has judged correctly but it is not one who desires the sheep. This wolf desires to devour the shepherd. Because I have likened him to a good shepherd, yea even a great shepherd,"

"What do I do, Lord?" I asked in the vision.

"What is that in thine hand?" the voice replied.

"A rod," was my response.

"Cast it down!" was the command before the vision closed.

I was amazed. This spirit had set out to destroy me in the flower of my pastorate. The command to cast down my rod was taken from Exodus the 4th chapter and spoke of the authority that Moses would use as he faced Pharaoh and all his sorcerers in Egypt, but I still didn't know quite how to interpret the vision.

The second vision occurred some time later. It opened with a clicking sound and the appearance of hands holding two knitting needles. The hands were knitting a garment incredibly fast. My eyes followed the single trail of yarn until I saw that it was connected not to a ball of yarn, but to the back end of a sheep. My eyes trailed back to the hands knitting ever so rapidly, and then back to the sheep which was beginning to show more bare skin as its fleece unraveled in a circular motion. Suddenly out popped this bushy tail! *A wolf!* I thought. My eyes focused on the bare flesh of the wolf and saw that it was full of sores and hideous mange. Again my eyes traveled the length of the yarn back to the hands that were now knitting at lightning speed. No one can knit this fast I said to myself, "no one but the hands of God!" The vision closed and the clicking ceased as I deduced its meaning: God was saying that He, Himself would reveal this sickly wolf.

Ironically, as I was having revelations from God concerning the evil that was in our midst, so was Jezebel. In Revelation, Chapter 2, Jezebel *"calleth herself a prophetess"* (Rev. 2:9). On two separate occasions I woke up on Sunday morning to hear the voice of the Lord say, "Someone is dreaming dreams . . . but it is not of me." Puzzled, I'd sit in church until testimony service when this individual stood up in the congregation declaring, "I had a dream last night." I was aghast. The dreams were false. Much as a peacock would spread its feathers to gain an audience, Jezebel was merely pulling attention towards herself. The weak, gullible and highly impressionable would be the first to fall into her web of self-deceit and divination. Only the mature could steer clear of her despicable charm.

As a confirmation, Holly called from England and shared an experience she had while she and a youth group were interceding in their church. She was transported up and over to our church in Canton while praying in the Spirit. She could clearly see inside and in the pulpit was a wolf standing behind the podium. She began to rebuke in loud, forceful tongues. The wolf scampered down the right aisle to the door and exited, but not before turning its head back with a snaring growl. Holly did not know what it

First Encounter: Jezebel

meant but I certainly did. Again Holly expressed her affections toward me and again I responded nonchalantly. This was not a romantic time in my life. I was in serious warfare for the ministry and for my very spiritual life.

Every move I made to improve or advance the church was opposed and misconstrued. I could not preach well enough, teach well enough, be anointed enough for this ominous force. The "where is the money going?" issue came up, and Jezebel was amazed that I did not receive one penny from the church. I plainly stated that I tithed faithfully and had the advancement of the ministry at heart. Though my integrity in financial matters was beyond reproach, the opposition only intensified. Again, she never spoke these things directly. Others voiced her dissatisfactions while she sat silent, but I knew that it was she who was stirring rebellion.

According to Jezebel, my effort to delegate responsibility was control. My bachelor status was a sign of perversion, and despite the anointing on my life, there was absolutely no way I could be a genuine man of God. My teaching was false doctrine even though it came straight from the Word in simplicity and power. God showed me that she would pass notes around as I taught, questioning the doctrine. I reflected on the opposition years ago from the women in BASIC resisting my position as Master of Ceremonies for the banquet. This too, was Jezebel. She was my thorn in the flesh from the very start!

The intensity of the battle with Jezebel became evident even to strangers. One Sunday, a visiting evangelist prayed for the members of my church at the altar after preaching a timely message. When the evangelist went to lay hands on this individual, she suddenly paused, stepped back and glanced at me standing a few feet behind. Her concentration had obviously been broken and she appeared flustered, but continued to pray for the line of people.

After service the evangelist said hesitantly, "Pastor Pugh, that sister with the blue dress . . . she . . . she . . . hates you!"

"I know," I replied in a matter of fact tone.

"No, Pastor Pugh, you don't understand, it's . . . it's no ordinary hatred. It's so powerful that I felt myself being drained. I turned to you for strength but you were standing back.

"I do understand. It's the power of witchcraft. It's the same hatred that witches have toward God. It is laced with brimstone. I can hardly stand it; this is why I stood back while you prayed."

We shook our heads in sad affirmation.

During Adult Sunday school class, I sat several seats behind her and commented on the lesson. She literally trembled in an uncontrollable rage as I spoke. My comments were met with a challenge, and for a moment it became a war of words between the two of us. The class looked puzzled, so I shut the debate down so as not to throw the entire lesson out of kilter. The hatred toward me had grown to an unbelievable intensity.

After about a year of dodging her darts and trying to keep such a low profile that one would wonder just who the pastor was, my bitterness worsened. I'd wake up Sunday mornings with one word in my heart: hate. I hated the ministry. I hated my job. I hated the very day I was born. Acrimony had eaten me alive. I was a walking spittoon full of acid and my ministry to the church was as defiled as they come. Of course, Jezebel discerned my fallen condition and used it to further her campaign to get me out of the pulpit.

As her followers grew so did my anger. I felt hurt, violated, and used. I stopped caring about pastoring. I merely went through the motions while carrying an invisible barrier raised to shield my already broken heart. With my bowels shutting up daily, I was living in an earthly hell. Only the children in the church kept me spiritually alive during this dark period. They were the only ones reflecting a pure love. I wanted out of the ministry, but God was sustaining me by His grace until He could give me some insight about what was happening within my own soul. Through divine providence, He taught me three unforgettable lessons.

Three Divine Lessons

The first lesson occurred one night as I sat in front of the television watching a segment of "60 Minutes". A young, third-generation, New York City police officer had been shot in Central Park by youths, only months after his installation. Escaping death by a thread, he was left permanently paralyzed from the neck down. In need of a ventilator to breathe and speak, he told his story with a sincerity that could cut through steel. "Aren't you bitter?" the interviewer asked.

"Nope," he gasped. "I blame society . . . what is a fourteen-year-old doing with a gun?" He spoke of missing intimate touches with his bride of seven months and regretting not being able to play with his soon-to-be-born son. He remained optimistic and forgiving throughout the interview.

I cracked and sobbed like a baby. Here sat a quadriplegic, having lost so much, without a tinge of bitterness; and there I sat, perfectly whole (from a physical sense), yet steeping in unforgiveness and rage. This ex-cop made no profession of faith but here I was a Christian, a servant of the Most High, sulking in resentment. I cried out to God that night from the depths of my belly. I knew I needed help, but didn't know where to get it. My only recourse was to quit the ministry and do a work for the Lord someplace else. I thought the mission field would be appropriate—any place in the world but Canton, Ohio. Like God sent the fish for Jonah, He was preparing the second lesson for me.

In the fall of 1989 I received a preaching engagement from two of our sister churches located on the islands of Antigua and Barbuda. Both islands had been ravished by hurricane Hugo only weeks before I arrived, and the islanders were rebuilding damaged neighborhoods and businesses, ever so grateful for God's mercy. From the moment I boarded the plane I grew weak and burned with a fever. By the time I reached Barbuda, the fever and chills worsened. The accommodations had vastly improved on the island since my first visit, but they offered no release to my acute sinusitis. I could not even enjoy my favorite dish of peas and rice with curry goat for my swollen gums.

After transferring to Antigua, things got no better. The electricity had not been restored to the island, so I had to read by candlelight and preach over a blustering generator. Each night I ministered with a diminishing vocal range to a sparse crowd. Afterwards, I staggered downstairs to a candle-lit basement parsonage. Sleepless nights were filled with a throbbing head, aching gums, and an abundance of mosquitoes preaching their gospel in my ears. I'd manage to sleep during the day, then muster enough strength to drag myself upstairs for the meeting before collapsing back into my prison. Though my voice was reduced to a whisper, God would miraculously restore it just before preaching. The physical and emotional suffering never abated until I boarded the plane, heading home.

I didn't need to ask anyone why I went through so much on the foreign field. God was telling me that if I didn't stand in the pastorate in Canton, this would be my alternative. It was a wake-up call to obedience. I had to gird up my loins like a man and face Jezebel. I ran back to Canton much as Jonah ran to Nineveh. I was ready to deal with anything in Canton rather than face the torment I had experienced in the islands. God had purposely made my stay miserable, for nothing teaches us obedience better than tailor-made suffering (Hebrews 5:8).

England

My third lesson and final wake-up call came again on the foreign field after I had finished our second international conference in London. The meeting was one of our largest and well received. Holly attended the conference and persuaded me to go to her home to meet her family. I wanted to stay in London but Holly's insistence was overwhelming. Under duress, I acquiesced and spent two days in Wolverhampton and the remaining days in London. I desperately sought out Carlos, desiring to see him and the family. Our correspondence had ceased years before but a phone number I had linked us together again.

When Carlos picked me up in South London, I was beaming with excitement until I entered the car. Carlos had changed. The fire was there but it had become a blowtorch aimed at me and any believer of the faith. My every reminiscence was singed into ashes.

"You're caught up in the past, Toni!" he said sharply. "The Word says, forgetting those things which are behind."

Carlos cut my every word up with a knife of vengeance and scriptures clearly quoted out of context. In fact he had vowed to let nothing come out of his mouth but the Word. A conversation with him was maddening.

Within ten minutes of arriving at his home I had been shredded into tiny pieces with a rage that made my blowup at UCI look like a serenade. I was slandered, belittled, berated, spiritually challenged, and insulted all in the name of the gospel. When I reminded Carlos that the fruit of the Holy Spirit was love, he'd suck up his wrath into one prodigious, fake smile. It would last only a moment before he would explode into another emotional fury.

When Dora and the boys walked in, I thought relief had come but things worsened. Dora looked gaunt and tired, the boys whom I remember being so vibrant, manly, and bright were obvious products of emotional abuse. The youngest, about twelve, sucked his thumb and rocked nervously back and forth while maintaining a downward gaze as I spoke to him. The oldest, about fourteen, was listless and mechanical.

Both acknowledged me but had little else to say. Dora smiled but immediately fell in rank as a soldier would before a commanding officer. Everyone appeared glassy eyed, exhausted and stripped of human feelings as do people who belong to a hideous cult. The air was accented with such an oppressive force that breathing was a major chore. The density was unbelievable. Like a mortuary, the entire house sadly lacked in joy. This was not the family I once knew. My heart was grieved.

Carlos continued his religious ranting amid my interjections. One thing for sure, though Carlos knew the Word by the letter, I knew the spirit of the Word and was able to tell him that he was clearly wrong based on various scriptures that I quoted verbatim. Eventually, he mounted the dining room table to get greater visibility and began screaming scriptures at the top of his lungs. The veins in his neck seemed ready to burst. I had had enough of this maddening scene. I bolted out the door and got only forty feet away when I realized that I was in a dilemma. I had no ride back to the house where I resided, nor did I have a number to call. I had come over to see Carlos thinking that I was with a friend; now I was stranded. Dora followed me out about the time he was yelling at one of the boys. His voice was resonating through the neighborhood.

"He's off . . . you know that don't you?"

"I know, Toni, but he doesn't see it," she replied.

"Don't let him do this to you, Dora . . . and don't let him destroy those boys, don't!"

I waited outside until she finally persuaded him to take me back to my destination. We drove back in absolute silence.

When I returned to Canton, the meaning of the incident was made clear. Carlos' state was but a mere mirror reflection of what I would become if I did not forgive from my heart everyone who had injured me throughout my tenure as pastor, including Jezebel. Appalled by his rage as I was, I could clearly see the same maddening rage in me many times while preaching in the pulpit during Sunday services. The hurt I had experienced made me justify my feelings but James 1:20 says, *"the wrath of man worketh not the righteousness of God."* God's word is inescapable.

I got the message loud and clear. If I did not repent and walk in love toward the congregation, I would be turned into a lunatic. The Holy Spirit later gave me a profile of the lunatic. It is the working of a religious spirit. Believers who possess the gifts and calling of God but lack the fruit of the Spirit (Gal. 5:17–22) are ripe candidates for this spirit.

When I returned to Canton, I fell to my knees at my bedside in deep repentance. As I confessed my guilt and renounced the path that stood inevitably before me, I felt something pull away from my spirit and travel upward to my throat. I spat out phlegm into the bathroom basin. I felt surprisingly free inside as though something had left my innermost being. Could this be deliverance? I grabbed the book, *Pigs in The Parlor* and quickly gleaned the chapter on self-deliverance. This had to be it. I began to bind the spirits of anger, bitterness, resentment, unforgiveness, hatred, wounded pride, and the heaviness around my spirit began to dissolve and travel up to my throat. Again I was spitting into the sink.

Miraculously, I felt even freer inside. My deliverance was slow and progressive. Not only was I in need of deliverance but God had to heal my broken heart, shattered through years of struggle as a pastor who only wanted to do God's will. I had fallen into a trap that many pastors find themselves in: retaining the hurts inflicted upon us by those whom we lead. When one is hurt he seeks to hurt others. If Bible forgiveness is not exercised, the enemy will have open access to torment us. I was in a spiritual mess and it was time to be healed. This process took months.

Much of my deliverance occurred on my job as I confessed resentment that had developed while under the gun of persecution and subtle racism. That Sunday morning, I fell to my knees in tears and apologized to the entire congregation for my bitterness and asked for their forgiveness. Jezebel had that "I told you so" look in her eyes, but I didn't care. I had to make right with my God and my flock.

The Holy Spirit did not stop with just my current conflicts with people and situations. He delved into my childhood and began giving me flashes of peoples' faces who had hurt me more than twenty years ago. I'd walk into the dentist's office or board the city bus and there they would be. God was granting me the chance to forgive and let go of the past completely and each time I did I felt wonderfully liberated.

The greatest freedom that one can possess is the freedom to love even his enemies. Such freedom places us on the same level as the Almighty God Himself, because God is love. The man who cannot love is spiritually bound regardless of his natural liberty. He may be free to come and go as he pleases; and if finances allow, free to travel the world, but if he cannot love, he is a prisoner within his own soul. Jesus came to set us free not only from sin, but sin's imprisoning affect on the human soul. If we stop at the deliverance from our sins only and not go on, we will fall into a category called stunted growth and miss a vast portion of a marvelous Christian life. It is the life that we enter into as we learn to love. Once again the Great Teacher was at the chalk board of my heart inscribing lessons that would last an eternity.

Chapter 6

THROW HER DOWN

Even after my public repentance, the rift between the congregation and myself remained intact. Jezebel had convinced many that I was the rejected King Saul. According to Jezebel, a young brother who had just joined the congregation was David, my successor. Jezebel was secretly trying to overthrow leadership from the pews, whispering damnable heresies and passing notes, encouraging him to take the pastorate. One night this brother picked me up from my afternoon shift and shared a dream that God had given him. Our pulpit held three large, beautiful chairs installed within a recessed back wall with a fifteen-foot arch. The remaining platform contained three tiers that stretched from wall to wall. The pastor's chair was centered and a foot higher than the other two chairs.

In his dream, two dead bodies were strewn across the lower platform floor. He was sitting in my seat and Jezebel was sitting in the seat left of him. He knew that something was not right. We talked until two that morning as I finally found someone with whom I could openly share what God began to term as the "mystery of iniquity." So deep had this rebellion gotten, that God would wake me up declaring judgment on the entire family, including the little children. "*And I will kill her children with death*," became literal in this case (Revelation 2:23).

I pleaded with God not to move out against them based on Ezekiel 18:20. I even told Him that I'd rather step down than to see innocent babies hurt. I received a stern rebuke: "Don't surrender leadership!" After all, the contest between Jezebel and the pastor is a contest of authority. Who will run the church? To surrender is to say, "Here, devil, take it!" God says, not so. He must raise up men who will not run, but face Jezebel in this hour.

The two dead bodies on the pulpit were Jezebel's eunuchs. They had been judged. Jezebel rarely speaks out herself. She operates in the shadows, whispering covertly against leadership while her eunuchs, those who have been seduced by her deceit, carry out her dirty work. They strike out against leadership while Jezebel maintains her camouflage. From this dream, we realized the seriousness of the rebellion going on in Deeper Life and vowed to watch as well as pray.

The time had come for our annual fellowship weekend with churches from Detroit, Boston and New York City. During our Sunday morning service God used a young female evangelist, who was not originally scheduled to speak, to bring this play to its final curtain call. She took her text from Numbers, Chapter 16, concerning Korah's rebellion in the wilderness and with an anointing unparallel to anything I had seen, began to preach and prophetically pronounce judgment against the rebellion in Deeper Life.

The witness within my spirit was so overwhelming that I fell to the floor and literally rolled off the three tiered platforms onto the ground floor.

"God will take your children out of here if you don't stop your mess! You better take your mouth off of God's leaders . . . these are the men who are praying for you . . . these are the men who are lying before God and laboring in the Word day and night so that you can be saved!" she thundered.

At those words I ran out of the sanctuary into the foyer. A deacon brought my glasses and wristwatch to me and helped me collect myself. After regaining my composure, I sat in the back of the sanctuary and watched as the evangelist went forth in God. Near the end of her sermon she, being full of the Holy Ghost, gestured for me to come to the platform. When I arrived, she took me by the hand and shouted, "Deeper Life, this is your pastor, hold him up, lift him up!"

At those words it was as if an invisible veil in the spirit realm was rent. One sister dashed up into the pulpit and flew into my arms, weeping uncontrollably. An altar call was made for our church and as everyone came forward, spontaneous weeping swept the altar. There, we embraced and mended a breach that had been between us for years. For years I had kept my flock at bay. For years I had avoided any unnecessary contact with them. For years I had closed my spirit to them in an attempt to shield my heart from the venomous darts of Jezebel.

Love is our defense to the missiles of the adversary. The shield of faith spoken of in Ephesians, Chapter 6 is a shield of love because faith worketh by love. No one gives you a manual for the pastorate with this information in it. No seminary can prepare you for the spirit of Jezebel. You must be enrolled in the school of the Holy Ghost. I preached, but I didn't love. My wounds were too deep, my heart too broken; my dreams for ministry too shattered. Only God could heal the awful mess. After healing me, He began mending me back to my flock that Sunday at the altar.

As I walked home that afternoon, God said, "Now that they know who the pastor is, it is time for you to be pastor. Go to your sheep!"

I set up appointments with every member of the church; some came to my apartment for the first time. There, I confessed my wrong and my love for them and many in turn confessed that they had been seduced by accusations levied against me to the point of not knowing what to believe. Jezebel was scrutinizing my every move and as for credibility, there was no way I could be a true man of God in her sight. I was irreparably flawed. That Sunday service was a reality check for us all.

When I held an interview with Jezebel, I spoke about God revealing that there was a wolf in our midst and that I was going to get to the bottom of the slander and accusations that were secretly being hurled at me. All offices were being suspended until the wolf and all allegations were brought to light. Like Joshua, I was through crying—it was time to search the camp. The following week the individual left with one of her eunuchs. That same Sunday our church offerings doubled! Can you imagine, losing members, only to see an increase in the tithes and offerings? The devil had been keeping God's people from giving.

We can never know those who labor among us by staying in the natural realm. Neither can we pastor successfully in the flesh. We must be fortified supernaturally, even as our Lord was, if we are to defeat the invisible enemy. Jezebel fled when I threw down my rod, a symbol of authority, because authority is all this principality knows. It despises men of God who will, like Elijah, execute the divine will of God in ministry.

Jezebel will undermine and dethrone the man who has the divine vision from God, at any cost. Scores of pastors are currently trembling under the fierce threatening of Jezebel. Many, like myself, initially have no idea of what to do. God had broken my sixties, highly confrontational, militant, in-your-face mentality to the point that I had become a marshmallow. I had left one extreme and gone to another. I should have taken charge long ago, but I was seriously out of balance in my leadership. God therefore sent others in to save the ship and quash the rebellion until I matured. I'm now qualified to speak on the subject and give unsuspecting pastors some strong advice.

Do not play patty cake with this spirit. Do what the prophet Jehu did in II Kings 9:33, and *"throw her down."* By this I mean meet her face to face, eye to eye, toe to toe. Don't back down. Put her out of the congregation if necessary, for there can be no peaceful coexistence between the spirit of Jezebel and men who will walk in the anointing of Elijah. It is a duel unto death. Let it be her death and not yours. Pastor, take your authority, for who will run the church is the real issue with the spirit of Jezebel.

This episode with Jezebel would be repeated many times. Each encounter gave me a greater knowledge of her *modus operandi*.

The pattern was the same. The woman would come in, loving both me and the ministry, then suddenly and mysteriously seek every means of bringing both down, usually through false gifts and whispering slanders. Some came in offering great promise to the ministry only to fall prey to this diabolical principality. Still others came in confessing their love for me in hopes of being a pastor's wife, only to retreat and seek my destruction.

We must view these women as victims. They themselves were not evil. They have yielded ground to a spirit that hates God's anointed messengers. It could happen to anyone. We cannot become misogynists. Our hatred is toward the spirit that uses them. Distinguishing between the two is paramount, for if we begin hating people, we too have fallen into the arms of the enemy.

Jezebel's end is described in II Kings 9:30–37. When Jezebel realized that her archenemy, Jehu, had reached the city Jezreel, she did not select a knife, but a mascara brush, lipstick and rouge as weapons of war. This speaks of seduction. She sought to reduce Jehu to a piece of bread by sensuality.

Many women came to the ministry under this same premise. At one point I absolutely refused to have any female in my apartment because of the powerful Jezebellian attack upon my character. Whenever a woman is seeking to seduce God's servant, she is a type of Delilah or Jezebel whose motto is, "control by any means necessary." God's servant should never be flattered at her advances or seductive charm—it is not you that she wants—it's your anointing and authority that's at hand. Samson had Delilah's undivided attention until he divulged the secret behind his strength. After he became bald, blinded and battered, she scampered off the scene with her money, never to be heard of again in scripture.

The most amazing aspect of the Jezebellian spirit is her ability to network and rally unsuspecting victims into her damnable heresies and rebellion against church leaders. I saw scores of people turn against me from one whispering lie. If she leaves a church, she will keep tabs through her eunuchs. Like robots obey the command from a remote control, so will these spiritually weak women and men obey her every demand. This is the power of witchcraft.

They become her pawns, spying and spewing out her grievances while she sits placidly by, feigning loyalty. They are caught up in her web of deceit for she is the black widow spider. So deep can be the entrapment that Jezebel can turn a woman against her own husband. "He's not saved . . . he's trying to dominate you," she will whisper while all along Jezebel is the dominating culprit.

At home, Jezebel will dominate, resist, argue and refuse to submit to the authority of her husband. It is rebellion. Wives must be careful here. Submission is an absolute principle according to the Word of God. When a woman falls prey to Jezebel, she will kick up her heels in word and in deeds against her husband and generally seek to rally others to her side. Such leaven will bring a marriage to ruin, for a husband will either fight for his rightful place as head of the household or cower down into a hen-pecked Ahab. Neither posture makes for a godly household.

The formula for a godly household is: husbands love and wives submit. Husbands nurture their wives and wives reverence their husbands. Such a balance will usher in God's blessing, but if Jezebel is on the scene the blessing will dissipate and forces of hell will pour in like a flood. Hatred and strife will permeate the environment because Jezebel hates male authority and strives against the rule of the husband. Secretly, from her heart she yields to no one.

The most dangerous aspect of the Jezebellian spirit is her unrepentant heart. "*I gave her space to repent of her fornication; and she repented not*" (Revelation 2:21). When our church was called to the altar that reckoning Sunday, Jezebel cried tears like everyone else, but before the service was over she was whispering slander against my rolling off the platform during the service. This spirit will not let the heart repent, but will use every form of deceit, rage, and denial to keep its victim bound. Such a state is most dangerous because God grants every Jezebel "space" that is, a season, in which to acknowledge her wrongdoing and come clean. This space is the longsuffering of God of which we are all recipients.

The heart of the Jezebellian victim can be so full of pride, vengeance, hatred that repentance becomes impossible. While she thinks it is God's leader whom she opposes it is God Himself whom she actually hates. You cannot despise Moses, but love Israel. Not even Christ can be held in one light and the church in a totally opposite light, for the church is the Body of Christ. We must not be too critical of the Lord's Body without offering real solutions lest we join the ever growing ranks of church wreckers. Jezebel must repent or meet with the judgment of God. This is a most serious matter. Women beware.

SIGNS OF JEZEBELLIAN INFLUENCE

Scores of women are unwittingly being used by Jezebel to bring persecution to God's leaders and the church at large, not recognizing that the church is the Body of Christ. The Corinthian believers were enlightened by Paul to this fact in the 11th chapter of the first book. Many reaped judgment, even premature death for not discerning the Body of the Lord Jesus Christ. Below are some helpful depictions of Jezebel. Afterward, we offer steps to extricate oneself from her power.

a.) Jezebel cannot operate alone. She must have an entourage. She befriends, bewitches and then betrays. Watch out for anyone coming to you speaking against God's leaders, asking you to touch and agree, or intercede. This is just a ploy to get you into the web.

b.) Nobody should be influencing your spiritual life more than headship. Jezebel will try to become a dictator to you on spiritual matters. I've seen control go so deep that one sister could not go to a revival meeting without first consulting with Jezebel. This is domination. It is witchcraft. She may visit your home and begin to tell you what is unacceptable. "These pictures are Satanic, get rid of them," she will state. You need never to make yourself accountable to anyone except God, your husband, and your elder(s).

c.) Jezebel will make claim to the prophetic to get the attention of the innocent. Beware of visions and dreams, revelations that bring injury to members of the Body. God never shows anyone anything to destroy another member of His own Body. Yet innuendo runs rampant in the Body because we do not recognize this truth, nor do we walk in divine love.

d.) Women are called to be covered by authority. Married women must be covered by their husbands. Spiritual issues should be discussed and agreed upon between them. If the husband is not saved, then eldership becomes the woman's spiritual covering. I believe that Paul's exhortation to the church of Corinth is a response to Jezebel activity. *"Let your women keep silence in the churches . . . and if they will learn anything, let them ask their husbands at home;"* (I Cor. 14:34). The Apostle Paul was simply reminding women of their God-given covering, their husbands. Single women are to be likewise covered, but in this instance by eldership. This passage does not exclude women from being in authority or in ministry. It simply means that they need covering. Deborah, a prophetess and the fourth judge of Israel, had two coverings. On the battlefield she was covered by Barak, the commanding officer. At home she took off her robe, put on her apron and served Lapidoth, her husband.

e.) Spirits of judgmentalism and criticism accompany the Jezebellian character. She comes into a ministry to judge it, to find fault and deem it inferior to her particular spiritual standard. No ministry will suit her. No pastor will measure up to her standard. The spirit of self righteous pride will be evident as she lifts her spiritual stance above all others with sayings like, "that's not right, he's not right, the pastor is off."

f.) Jezebel uses flattery like a baker uses flour. It is her way of winning over converts. Flattery is unduly or insincere praise with an ulterior motive. "Girl, you're so spiritual . . . God is really using you . . . let's get together . . . I see the power of God all over you." Such compliments are all means of seducing you into her web. The more you understand your own spiritual destiny, the less you are moved by people's comments, be they negative or positive. (Noah had little encouragement for years, yet he continued to build the ark.)

g.) She'll want to take you under her wing as a mother hen would her brood. Initially, this will seem wholesome, but it will turn into a nightmare of control and dominance.

h.) She'll come picking your brain to see what measure of the Word you have inside of you. She'll test your level of stability in God, mainly through conversation. If she discerns insecurity she'll move right in, but if she senses strength and independence, a strong reliance on the Word and headship, she will back off and devise a more cunning strategy to get you, sometimes turning the entire women's group against you. Those who are called into the prophetic ministry eat a daily diet of rejection and isolation so they will be highly despised by Jezebel.

i.) She will try to get close to authority for the purpose of control. When she is rebuffed or her suggestions in how to run the church are rejected, she will go on the warpath against leadership.

j.) Jezebel wants control of the house of God but can't get the victory over her own dirty laundry. Her house will be out of order. Her family life may be in shambles, marriage on the rocks, housekeeping in disarray all while she's trying to run God's house.

k.) The spirit of Jezebel comes against the minds of men and women and imparts imaginations of lust and adultery. Outwardly we may appear to be victorious sons of God, but inwardly we are in bondage to her.

l.) She will come against the pastor's wife with a vengeance because the wife serves as a covering for the pastor. She'll subtly or overtly try to turn all the women against the first lady.

m.) In some cases, Jezebel becomes the church bully, placing demands on the weaker women in the church, ostracizing them if they do not meet her insistence of controlling their spiritual lives or knowing their personal business. She will form cliques which likewise persecute those who walk independent of her demands.

n.) While ladies clubs and auxiliaries are good in their proper context, God showed me that caution must be exercised in this respect, lest spiritually young and unsuspecting women are sucked into the web of Jezebellian control. Women's meetings should be carefully monitored and plans for the group should be submitted to headship for approval. This is covering (something Eve lacked when she had discourse with the serpent). Women who are free (mature in this respect) readily comply with this rule, but those who are under the Jezebel influence will vehemently oppose such guidelines of accountability.

o.) She carries a spiritual barometer with her whereby she can "measure" the anointing on leadership. "Oh, that wasn't very anointed . . . the anointing was stronger this Sunday than it was last Sunday . . . Let's get together and pray that the pastor gets more anointed . . ."

In some extreme, but not uncommon cases, Jezebelism crosses over into the dangerous zone of sexuality. During our barrage of Jezebellian attacks, we had one sister who seized control of the women's group. Despite my rejection of her plans to have a "sleep over" at her house, she met with the women behind my back and set up one herself "independent of the church." The women were to come prepared to open up and talk about anything: their marriages, spiritual lives, fears, husbands, etcetera. No men were allowed for the weekend and though many women did not feel comfortable with the idea, none protested.

During this time God kept showing me the hunt scene on the wildlife channel on television. A pride of lions crouched stealthily in the tall grass as a herd of wildebeast grazed nervously nearby. The narrator noted how a stampede was caused by some of the lionesses, while others lay crouched down, eyeing their prey, looking for weaknesses within the herd: a young calf or a stray. When the stampede began, many darted right past the lioness without harm, for she had already singled out her prey.

Such was the case with this situation. It was a lesbian spirit that sought to herd the women together and sift out potential weaknesses. Once I discovered this rebellious plot, I rebuked the spirit, suspended all future women's meetings, and called the individual into account. Just as the rebels, Dathan and Abirim, refused to meet with Moses in the wilderness, so did she refuse to meet with me (Num. 16). Such are the actions of the rebellious. She left the ministry, anointed herself as pastor and started her own church at home. Again, this shows how desperate Jezebel is for control and rulership. Her pursuit of power is relentless. She will gain it by any means necessary. Fortunately, the ministry folded soon after it began because the word of God is alive and real, *"every plant which my heavenly Father hath not planted, shall be rooted up"* (Matt 15:13).

Chapter 7
THE TURNING POINT

My initial step into deliverance occurred on an unseasonably balmy December 24, 1989. Sunday service climaxed with an altar call where I prayed for a man named Roy. After the benediction, everyone retired to the basement dining hall for a traditional Christmas meal when I noticed Roy's absence. He was standing in the mid section of the pews shaking. As I approached, a supernatural fire ball exploded upon us and he was hurled to the floor and shook violently. I 'heard' the Lord say, "Call them out."

The next twenty minutes were spent binding and loosing demonic forces. Two brothers from downstairs were called to assist me by moving the pews aside. Roy twisted convulsively and choked up green phlegm each time a demon emerged. Those who were still in the sanctuary were astonished, but none so much as I.

After the deliverance ended, we all retreated to the dining hall for dinner. This was my first visible demonstration of deliverance with another person. I had done nothing to initiate nor to prepare for it. It was a sovereign act of God. I would later teach a class on deliverance and make this one lesson clear: deliverance is a sovereign miracle of God. No one can arbitrarily cast out demons just as no one can arbitrarily minister healing to a sick body. God initiates and expedites each move. He is the Author and the Finisher of every work. He alone can claim the credit and He alone can be glorified.

Our fellowship dinner lasted well into the afternoon but I had to hurry home to prepare for a dinner party God had told me to have. Nine guests were invited, two of whom were the brothers who assisted in the deliverance that morning in the church. God particularly instructed me to invite Eon and Henrietta.

The menu consisted of lasagna, green beans, garlic bread and a Caribbean punch. Roasted nuts, fresh grapes and a shrimp cocktail served as appetizers. Chris and Cheryl attended and both smiled when they saw the spread. Cheryl had just told her husband that she missed having access to the seafood so abundant on the east coast and there lay the shrimp platter. A brother named Ben and Holly were also there.

This was Holly's fifth visit to Canton over about a seven-year period. This time she came bearing a suitcase full of household items which I sadly lacked. Her intentions were obvious. She was setting up house, and while I was flattered on one hand, her aggression had become bothersome. She even pulled out some dresses and asked me if she could leave them in Canton. With an arched eyebrow I shot the request down. This was going too far. She said something about them being a few sizes larger for (there was a pause) when the children came. My frown was obvious. I gave her an unequivocal no.

By this time our relationship included more than a friendly embrace. Holly was persistent in receiving more from me. If I refused to kiss her (and I tried) she would begin to shriek and hyperventilate like she did that night at Sister Johnson's home. If I did kiss her, she would carry on nearly the same way. I was doomed if I did, doomed if I didn't. I had been in several relationships out in the world, but nothing came close in comparison to this one.

Though the relationship remained celibate, passion had seeped in. Her persistence overpowered my reluctance. My manhood got in the way. You don't pen in a wild tiger for seven years and upon opening the door, expect him to act like a kitten. The scriptures, especially Psalms 119:9, and my history with God, kept me sane and sanctified during this visit. Holly was as aggressive as any female wrestler. I was no angel, I assure you, but it was our love for God that kept things under control despite the fact that bonds had developed.

After Chris and Cheryl left, and the last cup of punch was gone, we agreed that it was time to pray. Eon and Henrietta had witnessed the move of God many times when we had prayed in the past, but nothing could have prepared us for what happened next. As we stood holding hands in a prayer circle, prophecy exploded from my mouth like a cannon and my index finger was in Eon's face. God was commanding him to kneel down. So forceful was the command that when I finally looked around, all those in the circle were on their knees. But Henrietta lay prostrate on her face. God spoke a stern rebuke and I, too, sank to my knees in fear, but Eon remained standing defiantly.

Just then, Holly pushed me aside, and finished the prophetical words of judgment mingled with mercy. When the anointing lifted, we all gave a sigh of relief, and gained our composure. Everyone left except the couple, myself, and Holly.

"Toni, I'm afraid for my husband's life," Henrietta whispered when Eon went to the restroom.

Eon entered the room before another word could be uttered and to dismiss any sign of whispering conspiracies I cleared the air with, "Brother, what's this all about?"

"Lying, Toni, my husband lies so much you never know when he is telling the truth. It's about to ruin this marriage," Henrietta interjected.

I looked compassionately at Eon. "Is this true, Eon?"

He confirmed this fact and upon asking if he believed that God would deliver, he retorted sharply, "No!"

"He'll do it for others, but He won't do it for me," he said with a sneering look on his face.

"Toni, this is not my husband speaking," said Henrietta.

I silently nodded. Eon's eyes shifted nervously from side to side. His nose pointed upward. I knew we were dealing with a spirit of arrogance.

I quickly escorted Henrietta out of the apartment and down the elevator to the first floor while explaining that little progress could be made in her presence. Upon my returning, Holly read scripture to Eon and he began to weep. The travail grew so loud that I got a towel and covered his mouth to muffle the sound. Senior citizens dominated the building and were quick to report noisy disturbance.

We sat Eon down in a chair and as he wailed like a little child, I gently began to call out the spirits. "You lying spirit, come out of him," I commanded. A surge of spit poured into the beige towel. "Arrogance, pride, you come out." Again he began to purge.

Holly assisted, by praying in the spirit while pacing the floor. She stopped and said, "call out lust." I did and lust came out. At one point Holly asked Eon had he ever stolen things as a little boy. He nodded, yes, and that spirit was cast out, along with rejection, loneliness, the spirit of religion, and several others.

Much of Eon's problem was rooted in childhood. When we finished, it was about 1:00 a.m. Holly went to Sister Johnson's apartment which was just two floors below mine. I took Eon home in a weekend rental car. I fell into the bed exhausted and exhilarated at the turn of events in my ministry. God was moving in such an awesome way. I drifted off to sleep by 2:00 a.m., only to awaken by a six o'clock phone call. It was Henrietta. "What happened in your apartment last night? My husband is not the same." Without going into detail I just mentioned the fact that deliverance took place, hung up, rolled back over and fell asleep.

I ran into Henrietta downtown some months later and she announced that Eon was a changed man. At first she suspected another feeble attempt at self-reform, but soon realized that God had done a complete work. We rejoiced in His name and departed.

Holly later asked me if I needed any further evidence that it was God's will that we be married. "You have a ministry, but it can't be complete without me. God pushed you out of the way." I gave an inward frown. No, God is a perfect gentleman. This was Holly's own aggression, an aggression that was becoming more powerful each time we were together.

God had an even greater experience in store that would literally revolutionize my ministry in deliverance. It all began when I awoke one Sunday morning to gaze inside an empty refrigerator and sighed. This was nothing new. Bachelorhood, pastoring, and a full time job left me little time to cook. I frequented the deli at Fisher Foods grocery.

After a great service, a young visiting couple, Dilan and Erna asked if I'd like to come home for dinner. In the car Erna said, "I was out in the parking lot when I heard the Lord say, 'He doesn't have any food at home.'" I chuckled and replied, "You certainly heard from God." Laughter and chatter followed us to their home.

After a spaghetti dinner we retired into the sitting room where an impromptu marital counseling session took place. Erna poured out her heart about a marriage spotted with rejection and emotional abuse. Dilan was a musician who spent many weekends playing with bands and she felt neglected. He played in a church where the musicians used drugs during the services. She got nothing from the services and stayed home.

Dilan despised her housekeeping habits and felt justified in his role as a tyrant in the marriage. Counseling went on for hours and tears flowed copiously down each of Erna's cheeks. Though there was no physical abuse, she had grown tired of being treated like a child. Dilan remained stiff and brutish, giving his explanation in harsh military tones. Despite his obvious wrong in the relationship, Dilan remained an adamant stone.

It was near midnight and Dilan refused to talk. When I motioned that I had to go, Erna jumped up and said, "If he goes, I'm going with him. Dilan, you're a hypocrite, you are a liar!" Her loud wailing sent me sinking back onto the sofa in deep concern. We had reached a stalemate. Just as I had given up hope the anointing fell upon me and prophecy came forth. My index finger pointed in Dilan's face, "Haughty, haughty, haughty" were the words of the Lord.

God spoke of his need to change in the marriage and of His longsuffering concerning Dilan's actions and sins. During the utterance, I saw a vision of a miniature Dalmatian, chained to a fence.

"Some treat their dogs better than thou hast treated thy wife," the Lord said.

Erna screamed in heart-rending anguish.

When the anointing lifted, Dilan remained impenetrable. It was as if the walls of Jericho had resisted even the shout of Joshua's army. I was in a dilemma. I couldn't go without Dilan; if I left, Erna swore she was leaving with the children. Silently asking God for guidance, He gave me this bit of wisdom.

"Dilan, get on your knees, look at your wife straight in the eyes and tell her to please forgive you for the way you've treated her."

Dilan did as instructed with the sincerity of a robot. Erna sat in a chair with her back rigid, gazing upon Dilan with great scepticism.

"Do it again," I said. He did. "And again, from the heart, Dilan."

He did, no less than six times. Then on the seventh time, Dilan's voice cracked and he began to sob uncontrollably.

The barrier had crumbled. I moved in quickly, commanding the demon powers to loose in the name of Jesus. We scurried to the kitchen sink, piled with dinner dishes, turned on the water faucet and continued deliverance as Dilan spat up chunks of Jericho's wall. After it was over, Dilan grabbed Erna and tearfully embraced her. They looked like two young lovers. Within that embrace was a godly sorrow for the years of unspeakable cruelty he had inflicted upon Erna. God had triumphed that night.

With a quick goodbye, Dilan dashed me back to my apartment. He inquired what had occurred and I told him that the spirit of pride had him so bound that he could not see his own wrongdoing. Only after he felt a genuine godly sorrow was God able to smash his pride to bits with the battering ram of conviction. The marriage was saved. I realized that from a standpoint of deliverance, divorce is seldom necessary.

When I arrived upstairs, it was after one o'clock in the morning! Ten hours had elapsed. My, how much God cares about His people. How little He cares about earthly time!

Chapter 8

AND THEY SPOKE

"He's changed," Erna said with sparkling eyes and a broad smile.

Dilan had come home that Monday from work and wrapped his arms around Erna in a passionate embrace. Women need lots of affection to keep marital inner tubes afloat. No measure of money, gifts, or lavish provisions can substitute for raw, spontaneous, old fashioned, meaningful affection. It is the glue to a happy marriage. If absent, the marriage is rotten from the woman's point of view. I said nothing about sexual expression here; I spoke of affection.

As deliverance and the prophetic word grew, so did the congregation. But with church growth came the crushing demand for more counseling and prayer. The sad part about it was that regardless of the time given to the masses, they refused to give back. Many fell away and returned to their former lifestyles only to darken our doors when a dire emergency arose. The church had become a glorified trauma center with a huge revolving door. We were dismayed as we saw scores pass through without assisting us in the church vision. Our numbers swelled and shrank each Sunday like an accordion.

I went to God on several occasions, chagrined and hurt about being placed in such a city as Canton, and the answer was always the same: "If the people would grieve thine heart, you, who have died for none of them, neither are any called by thy name, how much more am I grieved, my son?" Smitten mute by the sum of His thoughts, I sighed and continued in the grace God had bestowed upon me. But weariness was setting in and it was obvious to all.

I gave Erna the book, *Pigs in the Parlor*, and she decided to go into some self-deliverance but was interrupted by the children so we set up an appointment for deliverance in my apartment. This was not wise, but my motives were pure. I would later teach the team that deliverance should be performed in no less than pairs, with same sex ministering to one another whenever possible.

After a brief counseling session we stood and prayed and began to rebuke demon forces when suddenly Erna fell to the floor and began pleading with me not to cast them out. It was Erna's voice but the pleas were from another source. I could hardly believe what I was hearing, so I got a tape recorder, popped in a blank cassette and taped most of the session. The amazing part of this episode was that the demons who identified themselves and were expelled from Erna would represent the sum total of all the demons that we would encounter in the deliverance ministry.

"No Toni, no Toni, please don't cast us out. Let us stay in . . . please Toni" the voices cried.

"No, Toni, no Toni. Pity, pity, pity. Help me Mommy, Let us stay . . . let us stay, Toni, please."

"In the Name of Jesus Christ, I say come out of her. No pity, devil. Just come out of her now."

With that, Erna began to spit up and I raced to the kitchen to get paper towels. As I sustained a strong hand of authority, the spirits cried out all the more.

"Please Toni, please, I am a baby, I'm a little baby, I'm a baby, I'm a baby. Let me be a baby. Let me go back to those baby days let her stay . . . let her stay five years old."

Who are you? I demanded.

"I'm a baby, I'm a little baby . . . please Toni . . . let us stay" the voice said in the most childish tones.

"You spirit of infantilism . . . I command you to come out of her . . . loose!" The spirits came out screaming and pleading. Erna slithered around the floor like a snake. More pleading came. This time it was using deception.

"I want my parents! Help me mommy. Mommy. Please mommy."

I bound the spirits and again commanded them to come out in Jesus' name. There was more spitting and another manifestation.

"Who are you?" I asked.

"I want to be evil. You know me, Toni, I want to be evil. I want to be evil and roar. They do not know who they were messing with."

At this point Erna was on all fours, charging as a bull would charge a matador.

"Who are you?" I asked again.

"I'm a bully, Toni, I'm angry . . . angry, Toni."

I bound the spirit of anger and intimidation. I then took authority over the bully spirit. Erna wailed and collapsed into a fetal position all while spitting up globes of mucus.

"Who are you?"

"I'm tired. I'm so tired. Things she's supposed to—I tire her. Her husband does not understand. I tire her. She should have strength, but I tire her. She could do so many great things for God, but I tire her."

I took authority of the spirit of fatigue. Now I began to see what was causing some of the conflict in the marriage. Erna's housekeeping drove Dilan to the point of rage. Dilan thought it was rebellion, but it was the work of malevolent spirits.

I bound the spirits of tiredness, fatigue, and laziness. There was resistance but the spirits were expelled with cries and spitting. It was a good thing that I had the cassette going because I would not have believed it otherwise. The next manifestation proved to be quite interesting.

"Who are you?" I asked.

The voice and tone changed dramatically, almost sensually.

"Look at me. Aren't I pretty? Look at me, Toni. Don't you think she's pretty? Pretty, pretty, pretty. She's pretty but you just don't know Toni, she has low self esteem."

At that point I took authority over three spirits: the spirit of vanity, the spirit of flattery, and the spirit of low self esteem. Along with vanity, I called out the spirit of seduction which was trying to throw the deliverance session out of sync. This is why it is important for deliverance workers to work in pairs. The session continued:

"Who are you?"

"We speak to her, we speak evil and we tell her what to do. We tell her what to do."

"How many of them are you? How many?"

"We are many, she does not know the will of the Lord because we speak and speak and speak. We speak in her mind. We speak all day long."

I persisted binding and loosing the talking spirits. The session continued.

"Who are you?"

"I am witchery spirit. We curse her. We want to put her under a curse."

"You witchcraft spirit, I curse your curse and command you to come out of her in the name of Jesus," I said.

"Who are you?"

"I rule. Let her stay captive in my powers, in my hands. I want to rule. Let me rule this body this day. Let me have dominion over this body, Toni. I want to enslave her. I want her to be mine. I want her to answer to me. Her sister said, answer to me. I want her to answer to me, Sherry."

Baffled, I pressed for more information.

"I hold her. Let me rule. I'm older. I'm older. She is cursed and I said I want to rule."

As I called out the spirit of dominion, it began to protest.

"If you call me out, I will have to come out of Sherry and I don't want to come out. I'm the head. And I'm not the tail. Don't say it. Don't say it, Toni."

At this point I realized that I was dealing with an ungodly soul tie. I did not know the details as yet, but I began to break it in the name of Jesus.

"No. No. No. No, don't break it Toni. Let her stay. That's my only sister. Let her stay."

The deliverance ended in a cry that could curdle blood.

I began to call on the blood of Jesus and the spirits reacted violently. I had to hold Erna down.

"No blood, don't give us no blood. Don't."

"Who are you? What is your name?"

"Ha, ha Toni. Don't you want me Toni? Ha, ha."

"Who are? What is your name?"

"Lust, O. K. lust, lust O. K. Toni, lust. Lust O. K. Toni, lust. Lust in me, Toni, lust in me."

I moved back at this point.

"Loose."

"All the people lust her. They lust her, I want to lust her, I want to ravish it, ravish. I want to feed upon her body, She is strong, she is strong but I want to ravish her."

"You have one command, come out in the name of Jesus."

"Why Toni? Let her lust."

"She has nothing but love," I said, because lust is the devil's counterfeit to love.

"We lust her body."

"No, you lying devil. Let her go."

"We are in men and we lust upon her. We lust upon her body and we want it. It looks so good to us, to us. Her body looks good to us. We exist in many men, many men, and we want to lust her body. Please let us lust upon her body."

When I heard these words I was shocked. Sensuality was definitely not Erna's character. She was a godly woman, yet these spirits had been transferred from lusting men who found her attractive. No wonder God wants us to dress modestly. Spirits can attach themselves from the luring gaze of others.

I could recall a few Christian sisters in town who made overt statements of being believers: Christian banners and stickers adorned everything from their car bumpers to their office doors. They wore crosses, and carried Bibles, but all this paraphernalia was upstaged by false eyelashes, intoxicating perfume, heavy makeup, painted nails that matched the lips, tight blouses, plunging necklines, skirts with deep splits, rings on every finger and toe, and big weaves or wigs. The testimony screamed Christ, but the appearance screamed harlot.

Such mixed signals are a result of these kinds of spirits. This is why God gave Israel explicit instructions on dress. Clothes are to cover, period. Over-exposure, intentional or not, opens the door to gazes that encourage demon activity. The same applies with unisex clothing. It is taboo to wear things that pertain to the opposite sex (Deut. 22:5). Gender confusion can result, and in extreme cases an identity crisis develops that leads its victim into cross-dressing. Spirits are behind all such distortion of humanity.
After the spirits came out, I continued with the session.

"I want to stay in her stomach," the spirits spoke.

"No, in the name of Jesus, loose."

"You are not getting me out. I want to stay in there and hurt her stomach."

"No longer you foul devil. We cast you out."

"Cramps. We cramp. We cramp her, we cramp her. We cramp her every month. We give no mercy. We want to cramp her. We make her vomit. We existed from the young until she's old. Let us continue to hurt her."

"We loose her right now from menstrual cramps, right now in the name of Jesus."

Just then the tape cassette shut off with a snap.

"You taped us, Toni? You taped us? How dare you tape us, Toni. We do not want people to know that we exist!"

Had this not happened to me, I don't think I would have believed it. I was smitten. The session ended when the anointing lifted and Erna sat on the floor crying her eyes out.

"How could this be, Toni? How could this be? I thought I was saved," she cried painfully.

I gently comforted Erna with words. I told her that she was indeed saved. All the spirits were from her past. She had nothing to be ashamed of.

Erna confessed that she had attempted suicide after a broken relationship during her teen years. She also recalled playing with an Ouija board as a child. She spoke of having cramps so badly that entire days were spent in bed. I used this experience to help other women who suffered unnecessarily during this delicate time, including my wife.

Months afterwards, Erna remained cramp free. If I would ever doubt the reality of the session, I had the tape. Demons exist and play a diabolical role in people's lives, but thanks be to God for His awesome power.

Chapter 9

A Woman Scorned

By Holly's sixth visit to Canton our relationship had soured considerably. Her sweet, effervescent, jovial spirit had become critical and haughty. One could smell arrogance when she entered the room. She had quit her job as a chef at a posh London restaurant and was in Canton ministering. I felt no responsibility for her presence and attended none of her meetings held at various prayer groups.

When we did meet, I was clearly disdained by her and was subtly cut down along with every other pastor she knew. She intimated that my labor in Canton was fruitless without her by my side and to be honest, I partly believed it. When she left for New York by train I sighed in relief, but it would be short lived.

I was in the tub one Saturday in August of 1991, when the phone rang. It was Holly. She was as hesitant as I was cautiously cold.

"Uh, this is very difficult to say. I'm coming back to Canton."

I groaned, and she snapped back.

"It's not for you! God is sending me back to do a work."

I was given her arriving flight and received a call at the church during noon day prayer from the airport. Exasperated, I borrowed a car from Minister Moss and dashed to the airport. She was at the pay phone flipping nervously through an address book, looking for numbers to call.

I grabbed her bags, placed them in the car without saying a word.

"When are you leaving?" I asked.

"I'm not sure," she replied.

"Where are you staying?"

"God will have to work that out too," she said, "I have a one way ticket."

I blew up and a shouting match erupted before we ever hit the highway. Holly had flown from Gatwick to Canton without money or a place to stay. I was livid. (It reminded me of my daring trip to California).

At church, calls were made to various people whom she had met over the years but no one was available. One sister had received a lengthy letter from Holly asking if she could house her for an indefinite period. She had not responded and now Holly was here. The woman was fuming and flatly refused to take her in. Eventually the Mosses agreed to accommodate her for the night.

The next day, the four of us met at my apartment and talked. Like a beautiful mountain erupting into a violent volcano, Holly's words spewed forth like lava. I had never seen her like this before, yet, in retrospect, it was on the horizon. In rage she spoke of forsaking all to obey God and here I stood obstinate and unyielding.

Holly came to Canton with an ultimatum: marry me or else! She would either take me to the altar or to the grave. Her homelessness provoked many to take her in. After just one night with her, my members would become unresponsive to my preaching, disobedient to my commands.

Each Sunday, she sat in the church with her face as flint, exuding pure hatred toward me as I ministered. In her eyes, I was the reprobate King Saul, doomed of God for disobedience. She was merely watching the clock, waiting for a lightning bolt to slay me at any time. Sound familiar? Yes, Holly had come to Canton with full-blown Jezebelic poison racing inside her veins.

When Erna and Dilan had us over for counseling, Holly opened her heart. God had sent her to get married. She defied family and friends who begged her to stop chasing this American preacher around the world. When her younger sister fell sick, Holly ignored their pleas for her to stay home and continued packing. After one last, nasty confrontation with her mother, she left for Canton in a rage.

The very traits of strength, faith and courage that made her so admirable, were now yielded to the spirit of Jezebel. No one could tell her that she was wrong without being consumed by her fury. She had become an incorrigible monster. Sister Johnson was stunned by her transformation and no longer wanted to keep her.

Eventually the Mosses shared that Holly kept them up all night plotting during her stay over. "If he doesn't obey God, he is rejected and I'll take the ministry over . . . are you standing with me?" Talk about being shrewd!

As the war escalated, other women came on the scene looking to be a pastor's wife. At times they would gather together and I became every villain in the scriptures from Balaam to Judas. My prior history to this type of attack allowed me to stay meek and mute while carefully eyeing those being influenced by this ominous spirit.

I lay before the Lord daily in deep desolation and humility. There were no heroes in this sad episode. It was because of me that Holly was stuck in America with a vendetta. No matter how fiercely she slandered me, she could not charge me with immorality, and yet there are heights of passion that come shamefully close. I sorely regretted it all. While in prayer God revealed that I was suffering because I was late. "It is My divine will, My son, that thou be married."

While some are called into celibacy for the kingdom's sake, others glorify God in marriage and family life. I was behind schedule and grieving God with a single's life. I was doing what most men do, running from commitment, thus setting a terrible example to scores of young men who admired my status. What's worse is that I was a pastor which symbolizes a marriage between a shepherd and his flock. I was clearly out of order and God was clearly not pleased.

What He said next was a total shock. God revealed that He had indeed sent Holly, but not in her present condition. She had never let go of her bitterness toward men who had hurt her, starting with her father. And now I had joined the ranks of them whom she despised. Just by violating one principle of forgiveness, Holly had opened herself up to Jezebel. It was as powerful as I had ever seen. The Lord then dropped a bomb in my spirit.

"She will oppose the ministry," God said.

Holly's words were like surgeons' scalpels ready to emasculate every man in her path without anesthesia. I could neither be a eunuch nor an Ahab in a marital relationship. The union was doomed from the start. I sought God all the more.

When Minister Moss stopped by one day, I poured out my heart to him as I had done to no other. I was in the valley of decision. I needed guidance desperately. He said, "Well Pastor, Deeper Life is a church for the rejected people of the world. What greater testimony would it be than for you to marry someone of the same nature?" I solemnly shook my head in agreement and we prayed. Just as I was about to ask God for grace, He spoke an amazing prophetic word to me.

He said that He had assessed the situation and that I was a hard man to please, but that He would raise me up a woman who could do the work. In the meantime, He warned me of the dangers of being in an uncovered state. It was my season for marriage and Satan would send in counterfeits. Since they were already on the scene, I refused to be alone with any woman at any time.

Later, I had a vision of the back of a woman's head. I did not see her face, but she wore a pony tail and a grey plaid skirt. She was falling down to the floor when the vision closed.

Holly arrived in August and it was early spring of the following year. I had banned her from coming to church because of her disruptive behavior. Her defiance had created a pool of unsympathetic onlookers. No one wanted to keep her. She ended up staying with a family she met from another church.

Holly informed me that she could not leave Canton because a bag that her mother had shipped from England was being held in an airport storage company in Cleveland. The cost for its release was twelve hundred dollars. There had been a fifteen-dollar daily charge for storage since its arrival.

After divine favor and a full explanation to the company manager, the bag was released for the initial shipping cost of some five hundred dollars. I used a credit card and was handed what one worker said was, "the biggest suitcase" she'd ever seen since working there. It was humongous and incredibly heavy. When I arrived with the bag, Holly greeted me with a smile and thanks. I declined her offer to come in. Weeks later, I discovered that she had flown to Jamaica due to a family death. I've never heard from her since, but did hear that she was married.

Chapter 10

HE THAT FINDETH A WIFE

I was both relieved and disheartened by the ordeal with Holly, but one must forgive himself, and advance forward. God had shown His mercy toward me in promising me a wife. The same year in June, I flew to England for our third conference at Hodderstone. When Tim and Phil picked me up at Gatwick, I poured out my heart, describing my sad episode with Holly. I also asked them to forgive me for being such a poor example as a single pastor. Singleness was not the will of God. I was in rebellion.

When I spoke that afternoon to a group of eighty, my text was taken from the Book of Esther and her strategic placement in the Persian kingdom "for such a time as this." As the Spirit rippled across the audience during closing prayer, a young lady with a pony tail and a grey patterned skirt fell to the floor backwards. My Lord! God was moving fast! Maintaining my focus for the duration proved difficult because of her captivating beauty.

Once the conference ended, I stayed a week in London and asked God to confirm His choice. I sat in the pulpit during a weekly church meeting and glanced up at the balcony. There she sat wearing a little pillbox hat made so popular by Jacqueline Kennedy in the sixties. Later that week, a mother Ferguson had a group of us over for dinner and once again she appeared.

The climax came the day of my departure. An early flight out of Gatwick demanded a 6:00 a.m. wake up. Nine conference attendees took vacation time to see me off and she was among them. When we prayed in Tim's apartment, the power of God fell and I laid my hands on her and prophesied.

Yea, I say it, it is I
You hear it. I shall take thee, I shall remove thee miles . . . miles and I say it
And I say it shall be miles away
I shall prepare thee
And it shall be a quick work
My hand shall be upon thee in a mighty way
Then shalt I change thee, I shall change thee

She fell to the floor and I followed. The Lord then spoke:

> **"I say it to thee My son**
> I say it is for you (Alva)
> I say I am pleased
> I am ready to move
> I shall move on thee quickly
> And you have heard correctly
> I shall fulfill it—every word—every promise
> It shall come quickly
> I shall send thee around the world
> And I say it. Yea
> Miracles—there shall be miracles
> I shall work miracles
> —July 1, 1992

The anointing left us both on the floor, slamming our heels vigorously on Tim's living room carpet. While she and the others were mystified at what happened, Tim and Phil clearly knew what God had sanctioned. I wept uncontrollably during our mad dash to the airport and did so periodically while flying over the Atlantic.

I spent one day home before zipping off to a family reunion at my dear cousin Ida Burton's sprawling ranch in Tennessee. Upon my return a woman named Alva had left a message at the church for me to call her.

Alva was perplexed and wanted to know what the prophecy meant. Having just viewed a documentary on the plight in Ethiopia, she thought perhaps God was sending her as a missionary. Her soft, lovely voice did nothing to lessen her strong British accent. I had to ask her to repeat everything she said twice. I told her that I would pray for her and said nothing more.

When the phone hit the receiver, I was hit with a rebuke. God wanted me to move on it immediately. I called a week later and under her very conservative, short responses I cracked and backed out again. I had always taught against marital unions based upon prophecies, and here I was asking a total stranger from another country to be my wife. It took me a week to build up the faith and courage.

I called for the third time and asked, "I guess you're wondering why I keep calling you?"

"Yes," she said in a matter of fact tone. There was a pregnant pause and I felt my faith drop and fears of rejection arise like a mercury-filled thermometer in high heat.

"Do you have the prophecy?"

I wanted to break out into a cold sweat.

"Read it, please."

"You said that you thought that God was sending you to the mission field. You were right." A perpetual silence continued on the other end. She was not going to make it easy. My heart was about to jump out of my chest but I persevered.

"The mission field God is sending you to is Canton. And the only way you can come to this country is to come as my wife. So I am asking you to marry me."

My nostrils were flared from hyperventilation and only by God's grace I got through it. I waited for her response.

"I'm shocked!" she said. "Who am I to disobey God?"

"Now in my church I teach to never make a major move without seeking God for a confirmation. Ask God and let me know the answer. I'm home Saturday and Sunday evenings."

Alva called that weekend and said in an expressionless voice, "Pastor Toni, concerning your question, the answer is yes."

I was astounded. "What do I do now, Lord?"

I listened intently as Alva told me how God had been dealing with her ever since the conference. Her prayer and Bible study life had soared. She had lost interest in everything but God. She couldn't even participate in her youth group at church. No one understood her, not even her family. I told her that this was the work of the anointing, preparing her for her new adventure as a pastor's wife. The more we talked, the more our love for one another blossomed.

I set a date to return to England during the Thanksgiving holiday. Tim and Alva met me at the airport and after a day of rest, I met her parents to formally ask for her hand in marriage. Dad remained cool and agreeable, saying that it had to be God. But Mom took me through a grueling interrogation that lasted an hour.

"Are you married?" she asked.

"No!" I responded in a perplexed tone.

"Have you ever been married?" she asked.

"No, never."

"Do you have children?"

"No," I replied.

"I have prayed and asked the Lord to give me a reason to tell you no, but I cannot find any! I just want to know why do you want to take my baby away from England and take her to America? That is the real problem here. If it were in England, I could rest, but not in America."

"Have you got a wife?" she persisted.

I couldn't believe it. This question came up at least three times during the interrogation. I was beginning to doubt myself. I could understand their uncertainty about Alva's move, but I could not understand the marriage question. Mother was persistent in her questions. I told her that it was the will of God and that I had all intentions of getting what I came for. Things got a bit heated just as Alva walked in and saved the day. I really didn't know how to take Alva's mom whose last name, Lynch, aptly described what I had just gone through.

After a romantic dinner at the Belle Cafe, I placed a ring on her finger, confessed my love for her and asked her to be mine forever. While waiting for a ride home, I swept her into my arms and stole my first kiss. I felt that I was about to be raptured. Later, Alva explained that the daughter of one of the deacons from her church married an American soldier and moved to the States only to find that he was married to another. She returned home shattered. Since then, American men were shrouded by cynicism, hence the interrogation from Mom.

A March 13, 1993 date was set and Dr. Farrell agreed to fly in to officiate. The balance of the week was spent signing forms and complying with the rigorous British laws governing marriage. We had to hire a Registrar to witness the signing of the registry book. I had to stay 24 hours in Alva's Province, and there were some specific words that must be spoken by the Officiator in order for the marriage to be legal.

Departing was torturous. Alva was everything I could ever want in a woman. I wanted to be with her for eternity. When I returned home, I received a call from a woman named Betty whose mother attended my church and had died during dialysis. When I arrived at her home, Betty sat in the kitchen dangling a set of keys.

"You see that van out there? It's yours."

It was a beautiful custom-made conversion van with a lighted cross in the ceiling. I was awed. It turned out that Mother Stewart went to her grave telling her husband, "You remember my Pastor." Chester, her husband, wasn't even a church goer, but he followed me to AAA and signed over the van with a smile. The test was over. I drove home singing, "Have thy own way, Lord!"

March came in a heartbeat and I flew into Gatwick with my mother, my brother (going as my best man), a dear friend, Pastor Wade Bell from Detroit, and two cousins from the south, Ida Burton and Sylvia. It was the most exciting time in all of our lives. By the wedding day, we had people flying in from the Caribbean, Japan, and Canada.

After a heart warming ceremony, we entered a reception hall decorated for a king and queen. Lavishly catered and meticulously served, the atmosphere pulsed with music, excitement, aromas and tears.

Swamped by well-wishing guests, I'd peek across the room and witness lines of family and friends waiting turns to say goodbye to Alva. She was drenched in tears and me in guilt. I had derailed her whole life. In a few days, gone would be everything and everyone that she was familiar with. She was marrying a total stranger destined for a strange land. Her sacrifice was far greater than mine. Her obedience had cost her country, culture, family, friends, job, church, dreams and aspirations. She had become my hero of faith. I vowed that I would make it up to her. I'd give her the world if I could.

The reception began at two in the afternoon. We planned to leave by nine that evening but I couldn't pull her away. We finally arrived at the Conrad Hilton at 3:00 a.m., and that morning I knew my bride as Adam knew Eve. With a heart full of gratitude and passion, I marveled at the thought of what God had done. Though I loved Alva, nothing could be compared to my love for God. I fell asleep with Alva in my arms, God on my mind and a smile on my lips. Only heaven could be better.

When we returned to Alva's home the next day, she was again swarmed by friends and family. As time grew late, I grew perturbed. Though Alva had my name, it was clear that England had her heart. I consulted the Lord and He said that all would change once we left the country.

The following morning, Donald and Christine waited anxiously in the hotel lobby. We had overslept and were running seriously late. With Mom and Dad waiting sadly at the airport, we discovered that we were too late for boarding. As our flight was being rescheduled, Alva gleefully exclaimed, "Now I can go back home and see my family another day!"

"No," I interrupted, "We are not going home. Donald, please book us in a nearby hotel."

Alva's countenance fell, my authority bolstered.

"Oh dear, Alva and Toni must talk," Mom interjected.

There was little to talk about. I couldn't take another day of the tears and melancholy. Mom was forever weeping and we had to carry Dad out of the Hilton one night. Alva was suffering from a family soul tie that had to be broken.

We spent a marvelous night together and returned the following morning for our flight. Mom and Dad wished us off without sadness or tears. God had done something to us all. Everyone had accepted the fact that Alva Lynch was now Alva Pugh, a pastor's wife.

We landed in Barbados to the warm and welcoming arms of Alva's brothers and sisters. Our honeymoon was a special time and afterwards we arrived in Canton—the place of destiny. I carried Alva over the threshold of my apartment and introduced her to her new home. She was impressed until she went into the kitchen and found one pot, a spoon, a fork, two cups, and a dish rag. Of course it would never do. Twenty-four hours later she had transformed it into a real kitchen complete with the aroma of real food cooking. My, how sweet life was. God told me that not only would Alva be the desire of my heart, but that the marriage would be perfect.

I looked up the word perfect in the Webster Collegiate Dictionary and it was defined: "conforming absolutely to the description or definition of an ideal type; exactly fitting the need in a certain situation or for a certain purpose." God was right again. How could I deny Him? He doeth all things well.

Chapter 11

AND HE CHOSE TWELVE

During an evangelistic service twelve members were called out from the congregation for training and teaching on deliverance. They were given the name, the Vanguard because they were called to fight in the front of battle. Initially, I didn't know what to do with them until a mishap occurred.

It began with Kia, a backslider, coming to church after Tuesday night Bible study. Dangerously close to losing everything she valued in life, Kia wanted help, so I led her in a prayer of repentance. When I laid my hand upon her, she began to spit up yellow globs of mucus while praising God. At one point, I commanded the spirit of nicotine to come out and Kia coughed up a black soot that reeked of smoke into a white paper towel. After twenty minutes of deliverance Kia left with her face aglow.

It took Kia months before she could become stable in church—and deliverance was a continual process with her. One Tuesday night she fell out and began purging from demonic forces. A group took her outside into the foyer and prayed until someone said, "This sister has got to clean up her house." So six of them drove to Kia's home and went through her belongings as though they were on a witch hunt.

They rummaged through drawers, turned up mattresses, took pictures, removed her wedding gown concluding that it was "drawing spirits." Kia sat dazed and helpless as they carted off her items. I was at work at the time.

When Kia told me what happened, I was livid. An emergency meeting was called and I rebuked their crude and unwise zeal, and I demanded that an apology be given to Kia. Soon after the meeting, God showed me that there would have to be many more meetings designed to train and equip a deliverance team.

I had studied many books from men such as Derek Prince, Win Worley, Bill Banks, Maxwell Whyte, Bill Subritzky, and Don Basham. I spent one winter absorbing techniques and principles while strengthening my faith in casting out devils.

We chose to stick with the format from the book, *Pigs in the Parlor* on demon groupings with our own unique blend. Other reading material on the subject of demons was introduced to those who wanted to advance in the ministry. Mysteriously, many of the demons that we dealt with had been found inside Erna. The list is hardly comprehensive, neither do we consider ourselves an authority on the subject. God was merely birthing us into the deliverance ministry according to His sovereign will. When there was no anointing or manifestation, there was no ministry taking place. God governed all.

Beginners who are called into the deliverance ministry can benefit from this material, albeit our own experience in this area is somewhat limited. Soon after we began, we noticed a pattern in the type of bondage in this area. In one respect, it made it easy to identify the spirit and counsel the victim.

We experienced marvelous results in some cases, and fell flat on our faces in others. Although our church was located in the center of a high drug area, we had little success with drug dependency. Sadly enough, many who were set free failed to walk in their deliverance. I believe that this is the most frustrating aspect of the ministry, followed by the sheer hatred levied against those in the deliverance ministry. The very host of hell is marshaled against you.

By the end of the teaching session, the entire team had successfully cast out devils. They were amazed that the spirits were subjected to the name of Jesus. I emphasized humility and discretion, but delighted to know that just as the anointing on Moses' life was transferred unto seventy, a transference of spirit had taken place between me and the twelve.

The people in need of deliverance came in waves. Our Sunday services were stretching well into the late afternoon. We eventually established one night of the week for deliverance only. Those desiring our services would have to make it during Wednesday night at 7:00 or Saturday after noonday prayer. We refrained from personal appointments. It became too taxing.

If demons manifested outside of this time, we dealt with them accordingly, but we had to stop the invasion on our personal and family time. Scores were delivered from oppressing spirits. Marriages were saved, poverty was broken, suicides prevented, generational curses reversed, inner and outward healing received and retained, but there was just one major problem. The people who received so much from God refused to give back by joining the vision of the church. Besides this, the church remained pregnant with internal rebellion. I was disheartened. After a year or two, even members of the Vanguard began to falter. One member even lifted up his heel, slandering me and their work. This was no surprise for it was scripture being reenacted. *"Have not I chosen twelve, and one of you is a devil?"* (John 6:70).

Chapter 12

QUESTIONS & ANSWERS / MANEUVERS

Although deliverance was fairly new from a teaching perspective, I was amazed at how well the group received instructions. Everyone had either seen or experienced some measure of deliverance before, so there was no need to try to convince anyone of the actual existence of demon powers. Our main focus was to train and transfer so that the ministry of deliverance could proceed without me being present at every session. This is called mentoring. It is a vital and missing link in the ministry of the Lord Jesus Christ. Without raising up sons and daughters after our own spiritual likeness, our ministries will become extinct.

Even Jesus removed Himself from the masses to train the twelve. Had He not, the gospel could never have gone worldwide. But because of this principle, it was said of the disciples, Paul and Silas, *"These have turned the world upside down"* (Acts 17:6). This is the residual effect of transferring our anointing by means of mentoring.

In the mentoring process, one has more than just a teacher-pupil relationship. One develops a child-parent relationship. A teacher will not necessarily include a pupil in his or her will, but a father will leave his son an inheritance. This is why Elisha cried, "Father, father," before his mentor was taken up in the whirlwind. Elisha caught (inherited) the mantle of miracles. It was a good thing too, because a miracle was the only thing that could get him back over Jordan.

We do not realize the importance of this process. We must go beyond preaching and teaching and endeavor to train men and women according to our own anointing, gifts and callings. We are then assured that the work will not cease, even at our demise.

During training, we dealt with questions as best we could. Knowledge is power, knowledge is strength. It places one in a position of authority, therefore we should never stop learning, nor should we limit our scope of learning. We should drink from the well of knowledge covering all legitimate sciences, maths, history. The caution here is to keep all things in harmony with the Word of God, the final analysis of life itself.

Below we've listed some questions that we've been asked by the deliverance team and others.

Question: How do you know whether a behavior is a work of the flesh or the activity of a demon?

There are some seventeen works of the flesh listed in Galatians 5 including fornication, murder, envy and jealousies. Everyone of us are born in the flesh. It is the new birth that gives us a life in the spirit so that we need not fulfill fleshly lusts (Romans 8). Whereas the flesh works, demons drive us to do that which is evil. Impulsive, uncontrollable, "just can't help it" smacks of demon activity. The gift of discerning of the spirits helps in accurate diagnosis.

Question: How do demons enter in?

Demons enter primarily through the violation of a spiritual principle. Let's say that we tell lies all the time. The Bible makes it clear that, *"lying lips are an abomination to the Lord but they that deal truly are His delight"* (Proverbs 12:22). This sin can open the door to a lying spirit. When this occurs the individual is a compulsive liar and deliverance is needed.

I have also read of involuntary oppression of a person. By that I mean a person can get a demon by no fault of his or her own. A mother carrying an unwanted child can open the door for the spirit of rejection to inhabit the soul of the unborn child. The child may grow up with extreme introversion, a poor self image, and an inability to reach out to others. These are all offshoots of the spirit of rejection.

Question: How can Christians be possessed of devils?
There is a difference between possession and oppression. Possession speaks of ownership. When believers are born again, God has sole ownership of them through their spirits which are born of God. The soul realm, however, is so vast and has so many issues that demons may dwell in this area. This is demon oppression. By the power of God they can be forced to come out because the vessel now belongs to God. If a person is possessed, as in the case of the maniac of Gadara, they will be a person who is not saved.

Question: Once deliverance has taken place, can the demons re-enter?
Jesus spoke of this in a parable: *"When the unclean spirit is gone out of a man, he walketh through dry places, seeking rest, and findeth none. Then he saith, I will return into my house from which I came out; and when he is come he findeth it empty, swept, and garnished. Then goeth he, and taketh with himself seven other spirits, more wicked than himself, and they enter in and dwell there; and the last state of that man is worse than the first"* (Matthew 12:43–45).

Demons can re-enter a delivered vessel. I had one case where we cast out a devil from a dear brother just recently released from prison. The demons spoke through the brother, "We'll be back," as they stampeded out. The key to this parable is that the spirits find their former residence empty. I cannot reiterate enough how important it is to walk in your deliverance by steering clear of your sin and filling your spiritual house with the Word of God and the fruits of the Holy Spirit: love, joy, meekness, kindness, etc., daily. The most disheartening part of deliverance is the fact that many will come into the church, get set free, but then return to their life of bondage before the week is out. This revolving door syndrome is what began to drain us as a deliverance team.

Question: Can any believer cast out a devil?

According to Mark 16:17, *"And these signs shall follow those who believe; In my name shall they cast out devils,"* all believers have the authority to dislodge Satan from the premises. We have been given the keys to the kingdom which means we have authority over the enemy of our souls. Whereas all believers can cast out devils, not every believer has a ministry of casting out devils. Ministry speaks of a call, a centralized area of service. It is the same with the gift of prophecy. Paul tells the church at Corinth that they may all prophesy, but not all had the ministry of a prophet. A distinction must be made lest our zealousness take us into territory where the Holy Spirit has not led us.

Question: Do demons cause sicknesses?

The scriptures bear record that many malaises and sicknesses are caused by demon spirits, including fevers. We have had only a few cases where people received healing as a result of a devil being dislodged. We long for more.

Question: Can children have demons?

An emotionally unhealthy environment can open the door for little ones to be inhabited. Our homes should be havens of peace and God's love. Anything short of this can open the door for demon invasion. We had one case where a man was going through deliverance while lying on the floor. At one point, he began to behave as though he were having a seizure. I took authority over the epileptic demon and he vomited out a large pile of phlegm. Afterwards, I asked him had he ever had a seizure. The answer was no, but as a child, as early as four and five, he would see and touch an uncle who frequently suffered with epilepsy. Children should not be exposed to traumas and tragedies, for they can open the soul up to demonic invasion. Bill Banks has a good book on children and deliverance.

Question: Why doesn't God just give us deliverance when we first get saved?

We do get deliverance during the new birth. It is deliverance of the human spirit. *"Who hath delivered us from the power of darkness, and hath translated us into the kingdom of his dear Son"* (Col. 1:13). The soul of man, which is composed of the mind, will and emotions must go through stages of deliverance. If God would do it all at once, some of us would lose our personalities altogether. Deliverance is progressive because something must be replaced as something is expelled. Progression keeps the human soul from being devastated. Also, Israel was told in the book of Judges that they would drive out their enemy little by little so that God could prove their hearts (Judges 2).

Even though we may have demons, they cannot make us do anything that we don't want to do. When we resist them, we prove to God that our delight is not in sin but in His laws. Regardless of the measure of oppression, the Greater One lives in us (our spirit man).

Question: If we can cast out devils and heal the sick, why doesn't someone go into the mental wards and hospitals and clean them out?

The answer is simple. The gifts and callings are subject to the Gift Giver and Caller. We, as Jesus, can *"do nothing except what we see the Father doing"* (John 5:19). Everything is subject to God's guidance and divine providence. Many sick folk lay at the pool of Bethsaida, but only one man was healed by Christ. Why? The sovereign choosing of God. Everything is orchestrated by Him. Of course, human instrumentality plays a role. For example, if a person has enough faith, anything can happen. However, we are not here to bring God glory through our own cunning devices. God is glorified by and through our obedience to His Will.

Question: If demons do exist, why aren't there more ministries dealing with them?

One third of the Lord's ministry dealt with casting out devils, another third with healing. Certainly, the church has missed it on both accounts because Satan wants us sick and does not want his existence and role in the earth known. Exposure would be his doom. He came primarily through church theology and dispensationalized the deliverance ministry out, along with the apostolic and prophetic ministry—each which pose a tremendous threat to his kingdom.

Demon Grouping Checklist

Below is a checklist of possible demonic forces plaguing an individual. Remember, sinful practices can open the door to demonic invasion, hence, these practices must be confessed, renounced and forsaken if you are to remain free. (The list is in no way comprehensive).

➤ **Pride**
Self-Righteousness	Opinionatedness
Perfection	Self praise
Independence	Self recognition
Racism	Rebellion
Superiority	Haughtiness
Arrogance	Stubbornness

➤ **Dominion**
Manipulation	Bulldozing
Overpowering	Demanding
Bullying Spirit	Possession
Bossyness	Intimidation
Jezebel	Rape

➤ **Suicide**
Hopelessness	Belittling
Guilt	Self-Absorption
Self-Condemnation	Low Self-Esteem
Death Wish	Giving Up
Self-Hatred	Failure

➤ Religious Spirit
Extremism Delusion
False gifts Demonstrativeness
Lunacy Ambition for glory
Ambition for power Fanaticism
Criticism Ambition for recognition
Doctrinal Dogma Error
Exclusiveness Holier-than-thou

➤ Laziness
Sleepiness Slothfulness
Neglect Idleness
Procrastination Poverty
Uncleanliness Hopelessness
Tiredness Fatigue

➤ Fear
Phobias of all sorts Cowardice
Terror Panic
Horror Nightmares
Fright Timidity

➤ * Witchcraft
Astrology Palm Reading
Ouija Board Séances
Psychic Friends Black Magic
Fortune Telling Divination
Automatic Handwriting Lucky Charms

➤ Addiction
Craving / Drugs Food / Sweets
Nicotine Caffeine
Sex Gambling
Alcohol Spend-All

➤ Anger
Hatred Past Memories

Untrustworthiness	Murder
Hatred for women	Rooted Bitterness
Hatred for pastors	Violence
Rage	Unforgiveness
Wrath	Assault

➤ **Deceit**

Lies	Put On
Underhandedness	Exaggeration
Low Life	Cover Up
Hypocrisy	Sneakiness
Thievery	Pretender

*All occult practices are strictly forbidden by scripture and can incur a host of misfortunes when violated. (Deut. 18:10–13).

⁂

All occurrences during deliverance were kept strictly confidential—the exception being to gain new techniques, maneuvers for future training and teaching sessions. All counselors were trained to deal lovingly and sacredly with each seeker.

We dealt with demon manifestations next in our training session. Fortunately, no one was ever assaulted during a deliverance session. I cautioned all the women to have at least one partner present. We began ministering according to gender: the women ministering to the women and the men to the men. In this way indiscretion is avoided. If a male did minister to a female, another female should be present. Again, I was trying to avoid the mistakes shared by others whom I had read about.

When demons manifest, they are commonly expelled through three body gates: the eye gate, the mouth gate, and the nose gate. Scriptures bear record that deliverance is usually accompanied with foam, froth, and spitting. Mucus which resembles vomit is commonly spat out. When demons know that they have been discovered, it is common for the eyes to widen like the eyes of a frog. You will notice a sense of terror in the eyes of the victim because we really do have power and dominion over the demons. This frightens them especially when we use the name of Jesus and speak of the power behind the blood shed on Calvary.

When fear is not displayed, anger will manifest. This is the enemy's tactic to frighten the worker. Growls similar to those which would proceed from an animal are frequently heard during deliverance. I was watching the biography of serial killer John Gacy, the Chicago contractor who brutally molested and murdered scores of young boys. He would lure them into his house and through trickery get them to put handcuffs on. One young man escaped and testified that once he was securely handcuffed, Gacy unleashed a growl like a wounded bear before attacking him. That was undoubtedly the manifestation of a powerful demon.

Hissing sounds like a snake are a common manifestation. Sometimes the tongue will move rapidly left and right of the mouth when the demons manifest. I remember the case of a poor girl name Matilda. She came to the church homeless and penniless and without direction. After months of working with her, we got her a job and a place to stay, but little did we know that she had a terrible crack addiction. When we went into deliverance sessions, her tongue would move in rapid oscillations while she slithered on her belly like a snake. I can remember her calling me at night saying that every time she knelt to pray her tongue would move in the same manner. Despite several deliverance sessions and plenty of loving care, we were unable to get her to curb her appetite for the drugs, and I could no longer jeopardize my church with some of her erratic behavior. We had to let her go.

Forceful blasts from the nostrils when the anointing is on the person or when hands are laid on the head is another manifestation. Spirits are like breath, in fact the word spirit comes from the Greek text, breath. Therefore, heavy breathing from the nostrils and mouth is common. Also yawns, coughing, belching, or screams will sometimes occur.

Weeping may manifest when deliverance is on. I told the team that it is usually not the person, but the demon trying to win sympathy. Command the weeping to cease and press ahead into deliverance. They are crying because they have to come out.

Finally, the demons may speak. We may ask them their name as Jesus did with legion (Mark 5). By identifying the spirit by name we can hasten the session. Do not listen to idle chatter, pleading, or defiance. They are merely stalling for time. Command them out and do not let up.

Because so many would fall on the floor, we set individuals in chairs before praying. Stalwart and potentially violent men were placed on their stomachs for the purposes of control, should their movement get out of hand. Fortunately we have never had a worker hurt in any session. Laughter will sometimes occur when deliverance is taking place. It is nothing but the spirit of mockery. Bind it and cast it out.

Demon Manifestations

Frowns	Growls	Hissing
Heavy breathing	Rapid tongue movements	Yawning
Vomiting	Foaming from the mouth	Violent cries
Weeping	Fearful eyes	Angry eyes
Coughing	Mockery	Belching

I do not want to mislead you into thinking that every case of deliverance requires dramatic manifestations. I will never forget the time when I was browsing a book about the life of Corrie Ten Boom in Berean Christian Bookstore. My eyes fastened on a paragraph that described a demon being cast out. I felt that God was speaking directly to me and my chest swelled. I immediately began to look about for my first taste of casting out a devil. I recall going to church that Tuesday evening and the power of God descended upon me, taking me to the floor. When I got up, I was weightless, as though a millstone had been lifted from around my neck. I was astounded. No one called out anything, no hands were laid on me, there was no screaming or spitting, just a release. I was the one who needed and got the deliverance.

Maneuvers

Ps. 8; Mark 3:23–27 (key verse 26); Judges 7:19–23.

Binding and loosing is the most consistently successful way of dislodging spirits. Taken from the words of Jesus, it is the authority of every believer in the earth realm. Whatever we bind on earth, God will likewise bind in heaven. This means that the thing is immobilized. Whatever we loose here on earth, is likewise loosed in the heavenlies.

Binding the strong man speaks of dealing with the chief spirit. In our chapter on demon groupings, there is a chief or prince spirit which opens the door to other spiritual forces. For example, a person may speak of a compulsion to rule over others, to be bossy and controlling. We would first bind the gatekeeper, dominion, then begin to dislodge the various spirits.

The Old Testament serves as a classic example of spiritual warfare. The Lord showed me one in the book of Judges;

> "So the children of Israel served Eglon, the king of Moab, eighteen years. But when the children of Israel cried unto the Lord, the Lord raised them up a deliverer, Ehud, the son of Gera, a Benjamite, a man left-handed; and by him the children of Israel sent tribute unto Eglon, the king of Moab. But Ehud made a dagger which had two edges, of a cubit length; and he did gird it under his raiment upon his right thigh. And he brought the present unto Eglon, king of Moab; and Eglon was a very fat man. And when he had made an end to offer the present, he sent away the people who bore the present. But he himself turned again from the quarries that were by Gilgal, and said, I have a secret errand unto thee, O king; who said, Keep silence. And all who stood by him went out from him. And Ehud came unto

him; and he was sitting in a summer parlor, which he had for himself alone. And Ehud said, I have a message from God unto thee. And he arose out of his seat. And Ehud put forth his left hand, and took the dagger from his right thigh, and thrust it into his belly; And the haft also went in after the blade, and the fat closed upon the blade, so that he could not draw the dagger out of his belly; and the dirt came out." (Judges 3:14–25)

Here Eglon, the Moabite King, is the strong man. All of Israel was in bondage and under the government of the Moabites. Ehud is a type of deliverer. Left-handed though he may be, his oddity was by no means a deficit to him. God honored his courage and faith. Ehud knew that he could do nothing to the armies of Moab unless he first could "bind" the king. He used stealth and wisdom, killing the overweight king with a two-edged dagger. The king was fat because he had been robbing Israel of their fruit. Demons steal our fruit of love, joy and peace. The dagger is a type of word of God. With it, he killed the king, and escaped to rally the Israeli armies. A huge victory was wrought during his judgeship.

The Blood of Jesus

The Blood of Christ is the most holy substance that we can ever know. It has the power to cleanse the vilest of sinners.

I have taken the victim, and placed him or her at the foot of Calvary where the blood was first shed. The demons have cried out, "Oh no, not there, don't take us there, please." Sometimes I place them in the nailed scarred hands of the Master. This method has proven effective as well.

Civil War

This method is foreshadowed also in the Old Testament. I like the story of Gideon. It tells of the enemy turning upon one another in utter confusion after trumpets were blown and pitchers were smashed. The Canaanites were devastated by their own swords. I used this technique on a believer who came to church one evening looking for deliverance. He confessed to some sins that could not be mentioned, even in this book. I was not shocked but a bit saddened at how Satan has bound men in this hour. The need for deliverers specifically anointed for the maladies of men is critical. After his confession and repentance, we went into immediate warfare against the enemies with little results. Then I commanded the devils to turn everyone against another in Jesus' name. The brother began to spit up globs of phlegm as the demons stampeded out of him. It was amazing.

Quoting Scriptures

We have had the team repeat scriptures in succession until the demons were expelled. Scripture serves as a type of divine harassment which even Satan himself cannot stand up against. We see this in the temptation of Christ in the wilderness, where Jesus used the Word. Demons hate to be reminded of their defeat. They loathe the church who has the knowledge of deliverance. Below are some of the scriptures that have reaped us tremendous results.

> "And these signs shall follow those who believe: In my name shall they cast out devils; they shall speak with new tongues; they shall take up serpents; and if they drink any deadly thing, it shall not hurt them; they shall lay hands on the sick, and they shall recover." (Mark 16:17)

> "Behold, I give unto you power to tread on serpents and scorpions, and over all the power of the enemy; and nothing shall by any means hurt you." (Luke 10:19)

> "And, having spoiled principalities and powers, he made a show of them openly, triumphing over them in it." (Col. 2:15)

> "And they overcame him by the blood of the Lamb, and by the word of their testimony; and they loved not their lives unto the death." (Revelation 12:11)

"For the weapons of our warfare are not carnal, but mighty though God to the pulling down of strongholds, casting down imaginations, and every high thing that exalteth itself against the knowledge of God, and bringing into captivity every thought to the obedience of Christ." (II Corinthians 10:4–5)

THE POWER OF SELF CONFESSION

Whenever I feel a personal need for deliverance, I find a private place in which to pace the floor and confess any known sin. Then I begin to rebuke the forces of darkness. The results have been amazing. Confession is the gateway to deliverance and receiving the mercy of God. *"Whosoever hides his sin shall not prosper but whosoever confesses and forsakes them shall have mercy,"* (Proverbs 28:13).

I reiterated to the team the need for human compassion. Never were we to judge a person based on a manifestation. After each session we commonly hugged the individual receiving help. Erna was devastated. Some leave our sessions rejoicing; still others remain docile after it is over. Still others leave ready to wage holy war against Satan (instant recruits).

Our greatest problem was getting people to give back to the ministry. The recidivist rate was sadly high. Many would get delivered and quickly return to their bondage. Like the lepers healed by Jesus, one out of ten returned to help us with the work. Many others became vehement persecutors of me and the ministry. Only God's grace has sustained us over the years.

Chapter 13

PRIDE

Superiority	Untouchableness	Self-Exaltation
Dogmaticism	Haughtiness	Snobbery
Self-Aggrandizement	Unrepentance	Vanity
Boastfullness	Self-absorption	Conceit

ROOT OF PRIDE

The origin of pride is found in the book of Genesis. When man was created in the image of God, he was totally God-conscious. His adoration, affection, attention were focused solely upon God. God is not selfish. He wanted Adam to have goals and objectives so He gave him the garden to care for, and then the animals, and eventually a wife to love. Adam's focal point and consciousness changed dramatically when he fell into sin. The Bible said that their eyes were opened and they knew that they were naked. Look at Adam's conversation when God asked, "Where are you?"

> **I hid** myself
> **I was** afraid
> **I heard** thy voice

I was naked

Ezekiel gives us a glimpse of Lucifer's thoughts as pride drove him into rebellion.

I will ascend above the heights of the clouds
I will exalt my throne
I will sit also upon the mount
I will be like the Most High

Like father, like son. Adam took on the nature and character of the fallen Lucifer. Adam was no longer God-conscious, but became self-conscious. The preeminence is on self in a most sordid way and this is the root of pride . . . self-centeredness. It exudes from the souls of the unregenerated and regenerated man alike. Like pus in an infected sore, it oozes out to infect the entire area. It has so many faces that we hardly know which one will manifest next. There are:

wounded pride	don't touch me pride
I'm better than you pride	boastful pride
self congratulatory pride	holier than thou pride

The list is endless. Pride robs the glory from God and places the emphasis on self. God will not allow it. He will not share His glory with another. He therefore says, "*A man's pride shall bring him low*" (Proverbs 29:23), and "*Though He sits high he has respect unto the lowly but the proud He knoweth afar off*" (Psalm 138:6). And then there are the damaging effects of pride. "*Pride goeth before destruction and a haughty spirit before a fall*" (Proverbs 16:18). Pride will bring a man down in a most certain fashion. We as created beings have nothing to gloat or glory over. All things are from and by Him. If we have beauty, it is from Him. If we are intelligent, it is because of Him. If we are wealthy and renowned, it is due to Him for He "*sendeth rain on the just and on the unjust*" (Matthew 5:45).

The problem is that darkness separates us from the brightness of His glory. When we can no longer see Him clearly for who He is, we begin to focus on ourselves: our assets, our accomplishments, our attributes or, our shortcomings. This is when perversion begins. It is perversion because it is not like God! God who has no beginning nor end, neither has He anyone to give an account to; the Creator of everything has chosen to be humble. Can you imagine that! God is a meek God. Though He is Supreme, He is humble. Is it any wonder that He cannot stand the pride of man? This is why He wrote in Isaiah 10:15, "Shall *the axe boast itself against him that heweth with it? Or shall the saw magnify itself against him that shaketh it? As if the rod should shake itself against those who lift it up, or as if the staff should lift up him that is not wood.*"

I will never forget the time when the only theater left in downtown Canton, The Palace Theater, was being restored to its original beauty after talk of possibly tearing it down. I was in the area when God impressed me to walk around the building seven times, claiming it for His glory. Though I told no one about this adventure, inwardly I was gloating like a proud peacock, until I met a brother named Larry who said, "The Lord had me go up to the Palace and do the Jericho march." *Him too?* I thought. My bubble was burst.

I realized just how puffed up I'd gotten. Inwardly, I thought I was someone special, doing some special duty for God, only to find out that I was not the only one. I walked away thinking how this stuff called pride will rise up in our very bones! In Jeremiah, God said, "*Let not the wise man glory in his wisdom, neither let the mighty man glory in his might. Let not the rich man glory in his riches, but let him that glorieth glory in this, that he understandeth and knoweth me, that I am the Lord who exerciseth loving-kindness, judgment, and righteousness in the earth for in these things I delight, saith the Lord*" (Jeremiah 9:23–24).

We have nothing to glory in. All is from or by Him; we have only to worship. A true glimpse of Him will keep us humble. A closer walk with the Omnipotent One will keep our pride pinned to the cross.

The Proud Church

Proverbs 30:12, speaks of a generation of people. "... *that are pure in their own eyes, and yet are not washed from their filthiness.*" This refers to the self-righteous church; the holier-than-thou group who have used redemption as a class system. "We have the Holy Ghost but you don't." Words like, "We don't smoke, drink, or fornicate," is the mere boasting of the religiously proud. Any church which claims that it exclusively has "the truth" and everyone outside of its denomination will miss heaven is suffering from an unhealthy dose of religious pride. In John's revelation to the seven churches of Asia there is never an exhortation for believers of Thyratira to leave and join the church of Philadelphia, or for Sardis to take membership at Smyrna. Each believer is exhorted to overcome just where they are attending. It is the pride of man that makes us think that "we're God's chosen," "we have the truth," "God is with us and not with them." Many cults have perished under such delusion. Hidden underneath the spirit of error is the godless spirit of pride. Believers and church leaders must beware. Cleaving unto such notions causes rifts and schism in the Body of Christ.

Pride and Self will

Once we are saved, God determines to do two primary works in the believer's life. The first work is universal: to conform us into the image of His dear Son; the second is to achieve His purpose or will in our individual lives (Romans 8:28–29). Because so many believers stop at the forgiveness of sins and do not go on to surrender all to the whole counsel of God, scores of God's people are walking in self-willed pride. We do what we want to do; go where we want to go, without any regard for our divine purpose. Like Balaam, God must sometimes crush our foot against the mountain to get our attention, but even then, some of us never learn. This is the product of brutish pride. It causes us to become numb and insensitive to the delicate and obvious leading of the Holy Spirit.

As a result, we fail to be fully equipped and anointed for the end time battle. Satan loves to have it so. He is the instigator of pride because it will keep us barren of true power and lacking in blessings. Every believer needs to dip in the River Jordan, like Naaman, for the cleansing of our leprous pride. Jordan is symbolic of death to the self life. Remember, pride almost cost Naaman his miracle.

The Two Voices of Self

Today, we must be careful of two evil foes of the believer: the self-righteous self and the unrighteous self. The self-righteous self boasts on its laurels: fasting, praying, scripture quoting, religious achievements, soul winning. We become vainly puffed up that somehow these things make us secure and special in God. We thank God that we are not like others. It is our righteousness. This is the nature of a Pharisee, for the truth of the matter is that nothing we do gives us divine approval. It is all about what He has done, and our righteousness is from Him because it is of Him.

The unrighteous self borders on false humility. It spews out its weaknesses, failures, and confusions, and proclaims perpetual unworthiness. This too, is a pathetic show of the flesh. Note that in both cases, whether self righteous or unrighteous, the emphasis is on self. Self is the last frontier to be crucified with Christ. Self must go to the Cross, lest it proclaim itself king. Upon no other ground will you recognize the voice of self than in the crucible of suffering. Suffering will tell who we really are. Listen to Job as self cried out in the intensity of heat:

> He hath stripped me of my glory, and taken the crown from my head. He hath destroyed me on every side, and I am gone; and mine hope hath he removed like a tree . . . Have pity upon me,

have pity upon me, O ye my friends; for the hand of God hath touched me. (19:9–10; 21)

The Book of Job raises the age-old question of, "why do the righteous suffer?" Though God gives us no definite answer to this question, it is clear that through divine providence God extracts the highest form of glory to His name. If our self nature is delivered to a deeper death, if our vision of the Holy One is clearer, if we are elevated into a higher realm in both the spirit and natural; if we are enlarged, then our suffering becomes worth the weight of glory. Whatever our trial, God is dealing with the self life which is rooted in pride. As Adam fell from innocence into self-conscious bondage through sin, we may all be delivered to a God consciousness through the power of the Cross.

Personal Dealing

The pride of man is like the Euphrates, it runs both deep and wide, so intrinsic is this sin that it will take many years of the pruning hook, the fire, the chastening rod, and the fuller's soap to drive it from our being. After it has been dealt with, our only hope for sustained victory over pride is to humbly abide in the Holy Ghost.

God gave my own pride a fatal blow one Thanksgiving holiday, through a dear sister named Ann. Ann was a struggling divorceé with six children, four of whom were living with her. She came to the church absolutely destitute, unable to escape the rigors of an impoverished lifestyle.

The Sunday before Thanksgiving, Ann approached me and said, "Pastor Toni, I claim you for dinner. I hope no one has invited you yet. I'm cooking the usual Thanksgiving dinner, but you've gotta taste my best dish, sweet potato pie." God had flashed a vision of me donning a chef's white apron and hat, cooking in her kitchen. Discerning that divine providence was at work I accepted the invitation.

Ann was a pleasant person, but her lack of organization and authority made her home chaotic. Wasteful spending and lecherous associations would reduce a Friday welfare check to nothing by Sunday night. Barren cupboards and unpaid bills were the norm, leaving Ann constantly depressed. Eviction notices for late rental payments and untidiness kept her on the run.

The children, three boys and a girl, bubbled with excitement when I arrived. "Ma, Pastor Toni's here." I sat in the cluttered living room on a broken-down davenport, trying to avoid the visible springs peeking through its fabric. Ann's boyfriend was in the kitchen, spraying for roaches and cleaning out the silverware drawer where he apparently found a nest of them.

Lois picked up the cat and put it outside at her mother's command, then ran back into the kitchen to help with the food. I strained to hear water running in hopes that she'd washed her hands, but I heard none. I cracked and asked God for a release. My mind conjured up a million excuses why I had to go and, of course, I would make them as legitimate as possible. But God gave no release. As we sat at the tiny table, everyone expressed their joy of having their pastor over for such a celebrated occasion. But my heart was beating down in my foot. I gazed upon the turkey, potato salad, green beans, and ham. Ann kept boasting, "Oh, but the best is in the kitchen, Pastor Toni, nobody can make sweet potato pie like I can."

Though it was a cool fall afternoon, I was perspiring with anxiety. I looked at the knife and fork and cracked. I told God that this was too much. Suddenly a peace welled up in my spirit and we held hands, bowed our heads and said grace. I said the longest prayer perhaps ever spoken at a dinner table. I was binding and loosing and sanctifying everything, while looking for cat hairs. Afterwards, I cleared my throat in one last fatalistic pause, hoping that God would change His mind and somehow get me out of this situation. Alas, I finished the prayer and the meal was served. One would have thought I was a bird. I took the tiniest bites possible. All eyes were fastened eagerly upon me. They wanted so badly for their pastor to enjoy the meal. I prayed silently this time asking God for a special grace and special grace He supplied.

Eventually my staunch reservation grew relaxed as the anointing of God filled the room. My bird-sized bites turned into full-fledged grubbing. The food was delicious. As laughter and chatter abounded, the atmosphere became charged with joy. We began to feel the presence of God even more as I exhorted Ann about the reality of making every day a day of thanksgiving. Every day, she and her family could sit down around the dinner table and break bread. Every day there could be order and mutual respect. The more I spoke of God's plan for the family, the greater the anointing of God fell.

Soon I began to pray for the children. A powerful anointing fell and I called Erna to assist in the deliverance. God spoke many things prophetically to the family as the afternoon waned into evening. By the time we left, spontaneous praises were flowing throughout the house.

That Friday, I was off to New York City for a preaching engagement. While sitting in first class on Continental Airlines, I reminisced on what God had done. The Holy Spirit told me that I had passed a great test in divine providence. Like a grain of wheat that falls into the ground and then dies in order to bear fruit, my self-righteous, uppity pride had taken a fall on that Thanksgiving day to the glory of God. God spoke to my heart, "You see son, if you are to take my gospel throughout the earth, your pride must be broken. For there are kings of nations who live in squalor compared to what Americans are accustomed to, and yet they must be reached without condescension, or disdain, or superiority."

I smiled as the flight attendant gathered up the hot towels and placed the silverware wrapped in a beige cloth napkin upon my tray. As they were serving the meal, the Holy Spirit gave me a startling revelation. It was this type of first class setting that I was accustomed to. Throughout my life, I have eaten at some of the most lavish tables for Thanksgiving—tables containing the choicest china and silverware, impeccable table settings and exquisite meals, but it was at Ann's house where I celebrated my best Thanksgiving ever. For it was there that God came down in the midst with His anointing. It was at that table where the blessing of the Lord was rich, and the sweet potato pie was good, just like she said it would be.

An Altar To See

> "And when they came unto the borders of the Jordan, that are in the land of Canaan, the children of Reuben and the children of Gad and the half tribe of Manasseh built there an altar by the Jordan, a great altar to see." (Joshua 22:10)

This portion of scripture has great significance to us. Having passed through the perils of the wilderness and reached the brink of Canaan, two and a half tribes, Reuben, Gad, and Manasseh chose to settle on the eastern bank of the Jordan. This means that they preferred not to enter the promised land. Canaan is a type of the fullness of God. Jordan is a type of death to the self life and it also speaks of new beginnings. In order to enter into God's fullness in the spiritual and natural realm, one must be willing to die. They opted out.

Moses agreed to their request under the condition that they "help their brethren." They complied and afterward retreated to the Jordan and built a replica of the altar that was in Shiloh. It was an altar "to see." From its inception, every altar that God ordained was dripping with blood. It was never built to simply gaze upon. Believers must beware. The altar angered the ten tribes and nearly started a civil war until their intentions were explained. The issue was settled and peace prevailed; nevertheless, there is a deeper meaning here.

The "seeing altar" was unprecedented. Throughout history, beginning with Abel, Noah and Abram, the altar was built "to use." In the wilderness, Moses was instructed to build two altars: the brazen altar and the altar of incense. One dripped with blood, the other smoldered with incense (a type of worship and intercession). The incense traveled over the veil and rested above the mercy seat. From outside of the tabernacle, these altars could not even be seen by Israel. Yet in the Book of Joshua, the new altar is merely for show. There is neither blood being spilled, nor intercession heard.

The lesson is clear. If we build huge cathedrals and gospel centers where worship is mere entertainment and men are not repenting—then we have an altar to see. It is worthless to God. It is but the pride of man—a type of modern day Babel. When the enemy came in like a flood, these two and a half tribes, who wanted only the prosperity of the land east of Jordan, were the first to fall. It is better that we all cross over Jordan (a type of death to the self life, including to self-centered ambition) and possess God's highest and His best.

Chapter 14

TALKING SPIRITS

Gossip	Avalanche	Rumors	Blasphemy
Lies	Instigation	Talebearing	Reviling
Backbiting	Tell All	Talkativeness	Whispering
Slandering	Innuendo	Cursing	

During Erna's deliverance the spirits said, "We speak and speak and speak . . ." After studying this for some time, I realized that there were talking spirits that invade either the mind to mimic the voice of the Holy Spirit, or the mouth of an individual, causing their speech to be contrary to the Word of God. I've chosen to focus upon the latter because of all the sins that plague the church, the sin governing our speech is the most prevalent. The enemy knows that God is a God who speaks things into existence. He also knows that the world was created by the power of language. His aim has been to pervert the language of men to keep men from walking in the exalted levels of God. Look at the scriptures:

> "But I say unto you, that every idle word that men shall speak, they shall give account thereof in the day of judgment." (Matt. 12:36)

"But the tongue can no man tame; it is an unruly evil, full of deadly poison." (James 3:8)

"But he that shall blaspheme against the Holy Ghost hath never forgiveness, but is in danger of eternal damnation." (Mark 3:29)

"For he spoke, and it was done; he commanded and it stood fast." (Psalm 33:9)

"Even a fool, when he holdeth his peace is counted wise." (Proverbs 17:28)

"A fool uttereth all his mind." (Proverbs 29:11)

"Whosoever shall say unto this mountain, be thou removed and be thou cast into the sea; and shall not doubt in his heart, but shall believe that those things which he saith shall come to pass; he shall have whatever he saith." (Mark 11:23)

Because of the power that God has given to our words, we are literal walking death or life machines. If we speak things that are contrary to the nature of God, we release death. If we speak according to His word, life is dispensed. If we knew the damaging effect that wrong words carry we would speak very little. In fact, God has taught me repeatedly that it is better to say nothing than to unleash the adversary with wrong language (Proverbs 16:30b). Words are eternal. They do not die. They echo beyond the millenia. This is why there will be a judgment for everyone, saint and sinner alike, for every idle or unprofitable word that is spoken (Matthew 12:36).

We have prayed for scores of people, especially children, who are in bondage to the words of others. If we call someone ugly, then ugly becomes a spirit force that attaches itself to the person it is directed toward. From the very impact, that word begins to do all it can to fulfill its nature. It may try to make the individual feel unattractive, even though this is the farthest thing from the truth. During prayer we say, "I take authority over the words and the spirit of those words levied against this child, in the name of Jesus Christ. He is not a bad child. He is not a loser. He will not be a statistic. He will submit to God."

By doing this we block the curses that have been uttered. I say curses because this is what Balaam was hired to do to Israel by King Balak in Numbers 23:23. The word enchantment in the Hebrew text means "whisper." Balak wanted Balaam to utter whispers against God's people. Whispering in the negative sense is equivalent to cursing. This is witchcraft.

When we are operating in Kingdom principles we, like God, speak the things that are not, as though they were. In other words, that same child who may be unruly and in constant trouble in school, should be blessed by his parents. We bless by pronouncing a positive expected end on the child, regardless of the current behavior. This responsibility rested largely upon the father's shoulders.

If the fathers are absent from the home, then mothers need to know how to bless their children. The pressure in child rearing can be challenging, but if we bless and not curse, we will see the desired results upon our children. The frustration of daily child rearing single handedly can reduce one's language to perpetual shouting; however, God will grant the grace and peace for us to remain collected during trying times with our children.

Patriarchal Blessing

Near the end of each patriarch's life, the father gathered the sons around and performed what is now a lost art in the family household. They would lay their hands upon their children and bless them. The blessing covered inheritances, well-wishing, and if the patriarch were a prophet, then his blessing would cross over to the prophetic destiny of the child.

Having established this fact, now look at the scenario between Jacob and Esau after Jacob had stolen the patriarchal blessing from him:

"Bless me, even me also, O my father. Hast thou not reserved a blessing for me? Bless me, even me also, O my father" (Gen. 27: 34, 36, 38). Esau's cry is the cry of the human spirit of every boy and girl in America and across the globe. "Father, can you bless me? Can you say one kind thing about me? Can you believe in me? Can you tell me that I am special? That I have purpose? That I can make it in this life?" What is happening is that too many children are sent out into the world without the father's blessing. They have no launching pad, no positive root system. Note that the blessing came from the father. With the plague of absentee fathers in the home, the breakdown of the family structure, the rising juvenile crime rate should be no surprise. Scores of boys are loosed in life without nurturing words and comforting embraces of their fathers. Many do not even know who their fathers are, which leaves huge gaps in their soul makeup. These gaps will be filled by images of others. If the image happens to be a drug dealer, pimp, gang leader, or rock star, then woe are we.

God's Remedy

In our church, we have a special men's fellowship where we train and teach men on male issues from a Biblical perspective. Our aim is to produce better husbands, better workers, better fathers, future leaders and ministers. We have seen some remarkable results. We've had wives comment on the positive change. We can only take the nations for God as we reclaim our men and prepare them as leaders. Men are God's glory—women are the glory of men. If society fails, it is because the men are already failing. When Eve ate the fruit, nothing happened. But when Adam bit of it, the glory was lost, they saw their nakedness for the first time and God moved in for restoration, not judgment. If men are out of place, then women will become misplaced. It is time to restore men and then teach them to restore the family with and through right words.

God called Gideon a "mighty man of valor" while he was yet hiding his harvest behind the winepress from the Midians. He renamed Abram and called him Abraham which means father of a multitude when he was yet childless. God speaks the things that are not as though they are. When we do the same, we are operating in the God kind of faith. This faith ushers in God's highest and richest blessings. Positive faith confessions are not only scriptural but please God.

The opposite is also true. Negative words will usher in a destructive environment. We literally paint our world with our words. *"For he that will love life, and see good days, let him refrain his tongue from evil, and his lips that they speak no guile;"* (I Peter 3:10).

Since God created the world by His Words, His Word has recreative life. Man, created in the image of God, has the same power of life or death in his tongue. When we speak according to God's own Word, life is released with all its blessing. We can literally defeat the enemy when our language is in alignment with God's own Words. There is no other way. *"When the even was come, they brought unto him many that were possessed with devils: and he cast out the spirits with his word, and healed all that were sick"* (Matthew 8:16). However, if we speak negative words of doubt, fear, death and disbelief, we release the enemy into our circumstances and he will come only to steal, kill and to destroy. Abundant life comes to those who have a scriptural speech pattern.

Some cultures have slang and lingo that frequently cut down others, especially friends and family in harmless humor. For instance, if one was born with protruding eyes, he may be called frog. Or if one's skin color is dark, he might be nicknamed midnight. Culturally it is acceptable, but once we get into the kingdom such bantering is unacceptable because our words must become like His Words. Words take on life form, hence foolish jesting is to be put aside. When we are decreeing things and speaking to mountains, we have no time for idle words and jesting.

The Source of Bad Words

The condition of the heart bears the fruit of words. Words that speak evil, slander, revile, gossip or assassinate the character of another have their roots grounded in a bitter spirit. If our heart has been injured, it will show in our words. *"But if ye have bitter envying and strife in your hearts, glory not, and lie not against the truth"* (James 3:14). Envy is the hidden thrust behind most criticism and slander. No one wants to admit it, but pastors with small congregations find it easy to shoot darts at mega radio and television ministries. Many fail to realize that much of their criticism is rooted in bitter envying.

There exists also a terrible undercurrent of religious gossip where one leaks personal information under the guise of "touching and agreeing" or "I've got something for you to pray about." Scores have been wounded and much personal information passed off under this delusion. It is nothing more than the wicked fruit of the untamed tongue. The heart has not been seasoned with grace, for out of the abundance of the heart the mouth will speak. If we share the misfortunes and faults of our brethren, it is because we do not walk in love toward them, for love *"covers a multitude of sins"* (I Peter 4:8). One who tells others' personal affairs, even under the guise of prayer, is nothing but a talebearer and will bring great dishonor to the Body of Christ.

Moses' Mouth

For centuries there have been discussion and debate over Moses' miracle working ministry, his great mission, his misery, but I want to talk a little about Moses' mouth. The scripture says that he spoke *"unadvisably with his lips"* while at Mount Horeb and was barred from Canaan (Psalm 106:33). He spoke out of a hasty, bitter spirit and God counted it as rebellion. God, therefore left his successor, Joshua, some precious advice that is vital to us all:

> "This book of the law shall not depart out of thy mouth, but thou shalt meditate therein day and night, that thou mayest observe to do according to all that is written therein; for then thou shalt have good success:" (Joshua 1:8)

This was God's exhortation to Joshua. It is for us all. Meditation which speaks of chewing the Word repeatedly again until it gets down into your spirit and heart, is the key to what springs up in our speech. When I began the pastorate, my public speaking was impressive. I spoke optimistically and carefully. This came from years of meditating upon the Word of God. Then came the ongoing war with the spirit of Jezebel, then Korah, then Absalom. I fell into a pit of bitterness and vengeance and it was reflected in my speech. I was hurt and betrayed a great deal during this time. The ministry was defiled by my unwholesome words. I cannot express my pain and regret in this matter. I hope only to steer some other pastor clear from this deadening trap. When we preach to the tares, the wheat withers and dies. I am in therapy with God to this very moment. An injured heart is not easily healed, but thanks be to God for an unfailing grace which endures long.

The key is meditating in the Word and focusing on the Lord. Whatever is in our hearts will proceed out of our mouths. A heart saturated in the Word will produce rich, healthy language for the listeners.

> "Hear; for I will speak of excellent things, and the opening of my lips shall be right things. For my mouth shall speak truth, and wickedness is an abomination to my lips. All the words of my mouth are in righteousness; there is nothing froward or perverse in them. They are all plain to him that understandeth, and right to those who find knowledge." (Proverbs 8:6–9)

Chapter 15

LUST

Fornication	Adultery	Uncleanness	Masturbation
Homosexuality	Fetishism	Fantasy Lust	Voyeurism
Bestiality	Incest	Harlotry	Pedophilia
Burlesque	Promiscuity	Exhibitionism	Transvestitism
Butchiness	Effeminism	Transsexualism	

    The most amazing lesson God taught me concerning His love occurred one night as I joined Mike and Rita in some post midnight street evangelism. Armed with tracts and girded with prayer, we divided Cleveland Avenue up into blocks and went to work.

    As I worked the strip alone, I witnessed some of the most irreverent responses to the Savior's love. Some openly blasphemed God while flaunting their shameful lifestylse. In a fit of anger, one man flung his whiskey glass against the brick wall of the bar he was leaving while saying that God had let him down.

    My heart was filled with sadness as I witnessed the hardness of humanity toward our gentle Savior. While standing in the parking lot, my eyes caught a young lady leaving a car. She was being dropped off at the bar where I stood. I introduced myself and began to tell her my mission when she interrupted, "I already know you, Toni Pugh."

Taken aback, I took a closer look. She was unfamiliar. Dressed in a tube top and cutoff jeans she was obviously on the prowl. "Who are you and how do you know me?" I asked with a frown.

She smiled and said, "I know you through a mutual acquaintance of ours."

Flabbergasted, I peered even closer, scanning my brain trying to recall who she was. Her wig was slanted and makeup roughly applied, mainly accenting her already large eyes. I was stumped. I persisted in my inquiry. "Guess," she said. A bit perturbed by now, I let her know that I wasn't in for games.

"Your face will fall to the street if I told you. I'm Calvin," she said.

Suddenly, the scales fell from my eyes. It was a guy whom I knew in high school. We were on the speech team together and years later, went on a date with the same young lady one evening. I had seen him one summer downtown and he asked me if I would be a member of his wedding party. He was engaged to a New Yorker. Elated, I told him I would if I was in Canton that summer and gave him my mother's address. He was right. My face fell into the street.

"Calvin!" I said.

"No," he said, "It's Carla now, I'm a woman."

Sparked with debate, I said, "Oh no, you aren't."

"Yes, I am" he said. "Physically I am a woman."

Calvin informed me that he had gotten a sex change at Cleveland Clinic the day after his father's funeral (his father's bedside request). He said he was never satisfied being a homosexual. I asked about his fiancée from New York and he spoke of still loving her but having the compulsion to alter his gender. He said many more things, too personal to mention, that left me heavy and physically ill. The more I looked at him the more I recognized the real Calvin, and the more sick I became.

"If I got saved, will God accept me as I am?"

"He'll accept you as a son," I snapped.

"But what will He do about this?" he asked while giving a full body gesture.

"I don't know. That'll be up to Him. But He will receive you as He created you—a man."

With that, Calvin disappeared into the bar and I staggered homeward. The team had planned to rendezvous around 3:00 a.m. but I had had enough. My knees were weak, my head spinning, my stomach ready to retch and my heart was filling with disgust. Amid all these feelings grew an intense hatred for Satan and his plot to pervert mankind.

When I got home and fell to my knees I spoke to Jesus openly about my sickness, shock and disgust. Then I thanked Him for saving me from a life of sin and drifted off to sleep. The following morning I received a stern rebuke in my spirit. My attitude was wrong. I fell on my knees and repented. A sweet anointing fell upon me and I wept. Afterward, God took me on a five-month journey through His Word dealing with His unconditional love for all people. Along with the scriptures I read a little book by David Wilkerson entitled, *The Two of Me*. It was a brilliant piece of work used to canvas the gay district in San Francisco during the early eighties. I even placed a copy of it in the mailbox of the abandoned home where Calvin last resided.

The clock showed 3:40 p.m. and I zipped out into the chilled winter air toward the bus that was turning the corner without me. I missed it! I trotted three blocks north to the Third Street bus but it zoomed by. The wind gained momentum and flurries followed. I ran further north toward Tuscarawas where a final bus was bound downtown. It whisked by.

My emotions dropped. It was terribly cold, and I had lost valuable time. Certainly I'd be late for work. The Holy Spirit gave me a song within my spirit, but I refused to be comforted. My walk with God had been beautiful, but accented with a lot of pain. My primary suffering came from the loss of rights to my own life. God was in complete charge, ordering everything. Breathless from my brisk trotting, I crossed Cherry and Tuscarawas Street and just as I was about to step down from the curb onto Rex Avenue, I nearly collided with Calvin as he came around the corner. It was then that I recognized the providence of God.

"Calvin" I said, "did you read the book?" He nodded affirmatively.

"It was quite good," he said. Then he walked quickly away, as though he were afraid.

I looked back at Calvin as I had never looked at another human being before. From my x-ray-like eyes flowed pools of compassion and from my heart, rivers of endless love. At that moment, I loved Calvin so much, I felt that I could die for him.

As he scurried away, the Lord spoke to my spirit. "You have overcome this day." Tears sprang to my eyes. My heart leaped with an inexplicable joy. A great truth had been learned. We cannot despise any creature God has made in His image. All are created by and for His pleasure. All are His masterpieces to the world, marred by the enemy. It is Satan who hates mankind. We fall into the lowest depth of depravity when we do likewise. I was elated. The cold no longer mattered, neither did the wind. Yet another lesson had been stenciled in my heart by the Master Artist, and I arrived at work with time to spare.

DEVOE

Devoe came seeking deliverance at Deeper Life from a homosexual lifestyle. Though he was not exclusively so, (he had been engaged twice to women whom he truly loved), he felt a need to deal with the issues that frustrated his spiritual life. After a consultation, I began calling out all the spirits listed under lust only to have Devoe smile and then mock. The more spirits I called out, including the demon of homosexuality, the more Devoe sneered. He even laughed at me. I was obviously way off track. This went on for some time until I finally struck a cord.

"Incest!" I cried. Devoe drew back. His grin turned into an angry frown.

"All right, I have you now, come out of him you incestuous demon."

With flared nostrils, he began to shake violently. Extensive pressure yielded no results so we stopped to talk. Devoe opened his heart and told me about a sad case of incest with his older brother. As youths, the two shared a bed together and became involved for several years until his brother began dating young women. The brother eventually married and had a family, but Devoe was left with same-sex impulses that led him down a dark path of perversion. We prayed the prayer of forgiveness for all those who hurt him, including his brother. Then I counseled him on the tactics of the enemy.

Satan deceives the sexual active into thinking that promiscuity is an endless paradise of pleasure, never once telling them of the hurt, rejection, abuse, selfish demands, degradation and bondage that awaits.

I had Devoe lie on his stomach and place his hands behind his back. He told me that when I called out incest, he felt like grabbing me and throwing me out of the window of my seventh floor apartment. After deliverance, Devoe was freed from many spirits, including rebellion, bestiality and suicide. He had contemplated suicide throughout his life, but now he was very grateful to God for giving him every reason to live. He became a lifelong and a special friend.

Lust and the End Times

Sadly enough, God revealed some startling things to me concerning sexuality and the end of time. It is most urgent that we return to old fashioned Biblical sexuality. God is no prude—He invented sexual expression for a myriad of reasons, including pleasure; however, it is the unlawful expression of sexuality that will bring His wrath. I was shown a series of spirits being released upon the face of the earth by the legions. They were sexual spirits sent to bring identity confusion unto man. Their assignment was to infiltrate anyone who violated God's moral codes, regardless of their sexual preference. The Bible is clear: *"the marriage bed is honorable and undefiled"* (Heb. 13:4).

While counseling a teenager named Beth, God confirmed what I saw. Having been caught in a sexually compromising situation on school grounds, Beth's parents brought her in for deliverance. We cast out several spirits before a spirit was revealed by a word of knowledge named, "same sex spirit." Beth's eyes widened in sheer astonishment.

She was obviously 'boy crazy', displaying the unhealthy enthusiasm for boys that some young teens do when hormones are raging, but the thought of being with a woman had never entered her mind. The spirit however, was there, secretly lodged in the soul realm, waiting for the opportunity to express itself. After giving Beth and her parents a full explanation, they left somewhat relieved; nevertheless, the principle remained the same. Violation of God's moral laws will lead to perversion. The world is slowly being turned over to this vile spirit.

By the time that Jesus Christ will arrive, most of the world will be what is termed bisexual (Luke 17:22–37). As it was in the days of Lot so shall it be in the day of His coming. The men of Sodom were possessed with the most base spirits of sexuality known to man. There will be such a rise in homosexual activity that no one will be shocked. It will be the work of these wicked spirits. Along with this revelation, God said that they shall desire children. Pedophila will be on the rise as men are turned over to shameful and base passions. Even the church will be susceptible to them if we are not grounded in the Word. Our only covering from these malevolent spirits will be the marriage bed or celibacy. Any sexual expression outside these confines will open us up for infiltration.

The Case of Belinda

I sat in Belinda's living room listening to her explain her sporadic church attendance. Belinda was blunt and transparent, traits that made her so remarkable.

"Pastor, the thing that is keeping me from being in church is this one guy. I'm sleeping with just one person and it's hard to give up . . . but I do want to be saved. Oh yea, please don't say anything. I've been having dreams lately. One is about me getting AIDS. The others are about . . . me having sex with two ladies. Pastor, that's not even me. I don't like women, but in the dream there are two of them." She laughed nervously to ease her embarrassment.

I told her that this is part of the end time judgment.

"God is turning over people who are violating His sexual laws. Also, He is warning you about the consequences of your heterosexual activity. AIDS is a monster, Belinda. It's devastating. You have children to raise. It's not worth it," I warned.

We spoke a little more in depth and I encouraged her to come to church and stay under the Word. It alone can transform your life. It is a refuge for us all. No one is exempt from this heinous consequence.

Lusting spirits will enter every orifice of man. They will enter the eye gate and men shall lust to view pornography. (Pornography coupled with the music industry will be Satan's major vehicle to ensnare the souls of men as the end times approach). They will enter the ear gate and men will long to hear uncleanness, hence the multimillion dollar telephone sex industry that is sweeping across the North American continent. Lust will enter the anus and men will think that they are the organs of a woman, inserting objects of all sorts to gratify themselves, but will find no gratification. Likewise, lust will enter the mouth gate and many will practice the unconscionable.

We must return to Bible holiness, if this generation is to be saved. The change will be subtle but definitive. Already the gender line has become fuzzy and undefined. High profile athletes are wearing huge earrings in both lobes. What was once revolting, like two women mouth kissing on prime time television, is rapidly becoming commonplace. We are being seduced into a flood of filth and it has darkened the doors of the church. Lust will be the number one struggle of the carnal believer, as the enemy intensifies his attack upon moral purity. Our only refuge is an unfeigned love for Christ and cleavage to the Word of the living God. It is time for us all to find ourselves in Psalms 91. There we will find a rest from the inevitable.

Chapter 16

DOMINION

Control	Overpowering	Possession	Witchcraft
Demanding	Bossiness	Territorialism	Jezebelism
Manipulation	Bulldozing	Intimidation	Rape

The spirit of dominion causes people to assert aggressive force to take over that which belongs to another, be it a home, ministry, or even the human will. As the spirit manifested during Erna's deliverance, she perched upon her hands and knees and began charging like a bull. As I harassed the spirit with commands, I was able to glean the words that one would hear if they were dealing with the spirit of dominion:

"You must report to me . . ."

"I must know . . . I'm in control"

"How dare you go, do, say, this or that without reporting to me first!?"

The bottom line of this spirit is control. In Erna's case, her sister was a contributing factor in her already rocky marriage. Erna felt obligated to tell her sister every detail concerning their troubled relationship. This is never healthy. Her sister would act as referee, frequently berating Dilan, causing a tremendous resentment between the two. The spirit of dominion was drawing Erna into a subordinate position to her older sister, thus giving her sister control over the marriage. The spirit pleaded with me not to cast it out, because it would also have to come out of the sister. This was an ungodly soul tie, deeply intertwined.

We have dealt with countless cases where the spirit of dominion was at work. In the case of Ann, the spirit of dominion governed the entire home. By five o'clock Friday, every walking derelict and drug dealer in the neighborhood was shuffling about her house, few of whom she knew. Even though social workers had threatened to take the children away several times, Ann was unable to control her environment. This is the work of dominion. It makes one feel helpless to take charge of their own life. Ann's situation is common, especially in the drug world. Crack and dope dealers befriend young mothers living in subsidized housing. Before she knows it, her house is a crack den distributing to both local and out-of-state buyers. Guns, beepers, cell phones, scales and high traffic become the norm. The spirit literally takes over the household with children being the real victims.

To deal with such an invasion, one would have to receive personal deliverance first, then wage war against the existing spirits in the household. Help of a strong prayer band will be needed. Sometimes moving out of a neighborhood or away from the controlling person is the only workable solution. This is frequently the case in estranged marital relationships where the male is controlling and violent. Though legal action may be helpful, deliverance prayer is what will shut down the power of control. Once a person is free from control, the door to the soul must be closed to the aggressive demands of others or the bondage will recur.

A Thin Line

A thin line exists between counseling and controlling. In counseling, one gives a broader perspective into the counselee's situation in order that they may increase their options on choosing a planned course of action. The safeguard in counseling is that the counseled is free to make his or her own decision based on what information has been presented. In control, one is told what to do. The will is violated. The person is not given the opportunity to exercise his God-given right to choose. We must remember that God gave Adam free will in Eden. Adam could choose to eat from the forbidden tree as well as the tree of life.

Pastors must be careful. Our desire to see everyone succeed in the Christian walk can subtly be turned into domination. Even our insight and intuition on matters cannot lead us to thrust our will upon our parishioners. I have refused to marry people in the church simply because I did not get a witness that the union was of God. What I did not do, however, was forbid them to marry. I just told them what God had laid on my heart and left it with that. To insist that they do not marry borders on dominion. Not a few pastors have fallen into the snare of this spirit.

In addition, leaders under the spirit of dominion will want to play God. If parishioners go on vacation, attend another church, buy a new car, get a new job, they must report to the leader. If not, the leader will be highly offended, if not downright angry. Again, pastors must be careful. We cannot lord over God's heritage. People must be shepherded (protected), and grounded in the Word, then left to make their own decisions that will affect their lives. Even our children will have to be let go, lest we become domineering parents who rob them of the right of choice.

CARRIE'S CASE

One day we were at Carrie's house engaged in deliverance when she ran into the bathroom to spit up. The spirits began identifying themselves and said, "We tell her what to do . . . we control her . . . she must answer to us." As she spoke this, my worker had a vision of Carrie's father and sister. They were both Christians with Carrie's best interests at heart. She was a single mother, struggling to make ends meet and prone to make social and financial mistakes that left her in a pit of frustration. With suicide threats spotting her life's history, she was viewed as one in need of constant oversight. However, control had crept in and Carrie's will was being violated by her well-intended family.

For example, Carrie rented some furniture for an exorbitant monthly fee. It was beyond her budget and she would be broke before the month was up. When she turned to her family for loans they'd subsequently seek control over her choices, thinking that they were helping her. In actuality the spirit of dominion was at work and the spirit was cast out that day. Let this be a note of caution to all those who have great concern for others. Advising is one thing, but intrusion upon one's ability to make choices, even bad choices, can lead to the bondage of control.

Chapter 17

SLOTHFULNESS

Procrastination	Tiredness	Fatigue	Sleepiness
Neglect	Idleness	Low Self-Esteem	Uncleanness
Defeat	Failure	Hopelessness	Poverty

    The lazy spirit was probably the most prevalent of all that we dealt with within the ministry. It attacks its victim and makes them feel sluggish, fatigued and overwhelmed by the daily tasks of life. Every effort to accomplish something ends in defeat. Work amasses for weeks on end until the person cannot imagine anything ever being completed. Ultimately, the individuals accept their dilemma and even consider it normal.

    While dealing with this spirit, we entered the homes where the stench of rotten garbage mingled with other foul odors greeted us at the door, almost gagging us. Children's clothes were strewn all over the house. Empty food cans were abandoned on the kitchen floor with rats darting throughout the debris. In one instance, a dear sister began to throw up during deliverance and we could not find a clean towel in the apartment. In another instance, roaches were so dense that they were crushed underneath the soles of my shoes as I walked from the living room into the kitchen.

In each case the family had fallen sway to the spirit of laziness and had literally given up on cleanliness and order. The spirit creates a blind spot so that what is ordinarily offensive becomes quite normal. One woman had about a dozen cats romping about her home. I didn't enter—the stench was overpowering. Sometimes mental illness is a factor.

I taught the deliverance team never to cast judgment on anyone's living style. Say nothing. We are ambassadors of Christ sent in to do His bidding. We are stripped of our own opinions and judgments. I reiterated that once we left a deliverance session, we were to remain mute lest a door be opened to spirits of gossip, criticism, godless pride, and self righteousness. Also, I trained the team to offer assistance if necessary. At times our women have manned buckets, mops, and cleaning products, and have assisted in revamping an entire household. Mountains of laundry were cleaned and pressed. Instructions were given to mothers who never received home training from their mothers.

Casting out the devil of laziness is just the beginning. Oftentimes we must instruct the person in areas where they never received teaching. We cannot deal with just the spiritual side and neglect the natural. Jesus preached to the multitude, but He also fed them. This is the full gospel—a gospel which meets the needs of the whole man. This point was reiterated throughout our sessions and the team proved to be doers of the Word and not just hearers.

Proverbs gives us some insight to the operation and consequence of this spirit:

> "Slothfulness casteth into a deep sleep, and an idle soul shall suffer hunger." (19:15)

The spirit of slothfulness will link with the spirit of deep sleep and the persons under attack will find themselves sleeping most of the day and night. Ten hours in bed is abnormal. The individual is either physically or emotionally sick, or under attack. I taught the team to go through a brief history check before rushing into deliverance. Every condition is clearly not demonic. Nevertheless, God

Slothfulness 157

has an answer to every condition which robs Him of His glory in men.

Erna fell into this category. She would begin to clean her house but suddenly feel a deadening fatigue. Overcome with drowsiness, she would stop her household chores to rest, and never get around to completing what she had begun. Of course, the next day brought out new challenges and duties without the previous being finished. As chores surmounted, these spirits will do one of the two:

1) Cause the person to slip into a depression
2) Create a self-acceptance with the unclean environment

Both are conditions of spiritual sleep. Deliverance is the first step of waking out of this comatose state. Instruction and assistance may be needed to maintain the deliverance.

"The slothful man saith, There is a lion without; I shall be slain in the streets." (Proverbs 22:13)

Outside of medical reasons, an inordinate amount of time indoors can be a sign that one is under the spirit of slothfulness. Enclosure can be a symptom of many illnesses, mental and otherwise, but sometimes it is merely the working of demonic forces. Nature was created by God to be enjoyed and to reflect His glory. Jesus referred to nature throughout His ministry, primarily in His parables. Through parallels of nature, God teaches many lessons about life as well as ourselves. The spirit of slothfulness will produce a cave man mentality. The individual goes into his dwelling and scarcely sees the sun. Often television becomes the center of affection, which is idolatry, and the soul sinks into darkness.

I John makes it clear, that if we walk in darkness and say that we have fellowship with Him we lie (1:6). The aim of all demonic spirits is to dishonor God and cause a person to miss his purpose and full potential in life. The slothful spirit will descend upon an entire community where lawns are unkept, weeds abound, garbage is strewn about, and idleness is the norm. When youth are under the spell of this spirit, they will be prone to mischief. If they are not actively engaged in work or supervised recreation, evil spirits will sweep them away on the path of criminal behavior.

The major problem with low economic developments is that people with the same problems are herded together with few examples, role models or options. There are no visible exceptions to their current state of existence. The environment becomes a cave. Unless the church goes in with a message of deliverance, faith, prosperity and hope, scores will have their God-given abilities stifled, never rising to their fullest potential in life.

> "The desire of the slothful killeth him; for his hands refuse to labor." (Proverbs 21:25)

Poverty and slothfulness are commonly linked. One can be, but is not exclusively, the direct cause of the other. There are some clear exceptions, however. For example, there are entire nations of hard-working people who are impoverished. Because the land does not yield a harvest or the weather is not conducive to agriculture and livestock, starvation and poverty result, despite many willing workers. Solomon is referring to the individual who refuses to work. The person who sleeps long and hard is destined to a life of meagerness.

The three weeks that I arose at 6:00 a.m. were God's rebuke to the spirit of slothfulness. It was an effortless deliverance, much like being in a sail boat in smooth, gentle winds. The day that I didn't wake up at 6:00 a.m. was God now putting the ball in my court. I was no longer on a sail boat, but in a row boat. It was time to use muscles, exercise my will and determination, and row. I had gone from divine discipline to self-discipline. I could fall back into the old habits or I could resist, fight and triumph over this spirit once and for all. God gave me abundant grace to help.

> "And the Lord said unto Moses, Rise up early in the morning, and stand before Pharaoh; lo, he cometh forth to the water; and say unto him, Thus saith the Lord, Let my people go, that they may serve me." (Exodus 8:20)

> "And Abraham rose up early in the morning, and saddled his ass, and took two of his young men with him, and Isaac his son, and clave the wood for the burnt offering, and rose up, and went unto the place of which God had told him." (Genesis 22:3)

> "To hearken to the words of my servants, the prophets, whom I sent unto you, both rising up early, and sending them, but ye have not hearkened." (Jer. 26:5)

Arising early slays the carnal man who loves to sleep. God also showed me something in the Book of Joshua. We had been asking God how to take the city of Canton. The conquest of Jericho is a paragon of the church taking any city that is under the enemy's domain. The first thing I noticed was divine order. Instructions were given with specifications. Joshua needed only to obey. Though we wrestle against principalities and powers, we can only win as we obey the commander-in-chief. We must move out when He says and the way He says. The compassing of Jericho speaks of a type of intercessory prayer. The blowing of the ram's horn speaks of warfare worship. The silence speaks of discipline. And all this was done, "rising up early." Later we discover that Joshua met the devil at dawn which is the break of day, 6:00 a.m. (Joshua 6:15).

As I said, this was the hour God had awakened me consecutively for three weeks back in Irvine. This was also the time we met for our daily prayer band. God was giving us a soul per week. After my graduation, BASIC exploded in growth to some two hundred believers. I was awed. Students were being saved or reclaimed in record numbers. We had discovered when to meet the enemy and how to pull down the strongholds over a region.

Chapter 18

THE RELIGIOUS SPIRIT

Pride	Error	Doctrinal Dogma
Extremism	False light	False gifts of the Spirit
Preeminence	Ambition for glory	False Religions
Legalism	Ambition for recognition	Self-Righteousness

The religious spirit keeps a person from having a scriptural foundation with God and His Word. It loves forms and fashions of godliness without delivering the real goods. People who are involved in cults are classic victims of these wicked spirits. They love to mimic God and deceive people into believing that they are worshiping and serving God. Our only defense from such an imitation of the Holy Spirit is staying as close to the Word of God as possible. Wide swings to the left or right can be an invitation to this malevolent host.

Unlike many other spirits, the religious spirit does not necessarily entice us to sin. They will encourage you to pray, fast, read your Bible, even live a holy life as long as they can steer you clear of a real relationship with God through His Son, Jesus Christ. They will push the believer into delusion or an extremism that will be contrary to God's life or His Word. They are behind the hordes of unchurched members in the Body of Christ today. Some have been hurt. Still others deem themselves far above the teaching and activities of a local Body and isolate themselves.

My most memorable encounter with this spirit was with Carlos of London. After him, I encountered many cases throughout my travels and my tenure as a pastor. Again, this spirit is insidious because it seeks to deceive people into thinking they have a relationship with the Most High.

Another case in England was with a dear couple and their daughter with whom I stayed during my first conference. Richard was as pleasant as any person could be and his wife, Mary, was courteous and kind. Richard was well pleased with the conference and was eager to show me his collection of religious books. From a bureau he pulled out no less than six Bibles from other religions including the Koran, the Mormon Bible, and the New World Translation. His rapid speech and thick West Indian accent made it hard to discern his words, but the fact that he had swallowed error was loud and clear. He even spoke of having meetings with the Jehovah's Witnesses to debate the scripture. Along with the books were pamphlets, pictures, and the whole gambit of religious paraphernalia.

Richard was under the sway of religious spirits. When I returned to his home after our second conference in England, Richard had changed. He had become critical and judgmental. There was a haughtiness in his character that was not there before. He and Mary had gone through some serious marital problems and she had left him at one point but had returned. The Lord revealed that it was due to the abominations that were in the house. When they attended my wedding, I told him to destroy all the books and artifacts, then instructed him how to bind and command the spirit forces out of his household.

As I grew in grace and the knowledge of the ministry, I learned some vital facts about this spirit. There are four ways believers fall under the influence of a religious spirit:

The Religious Spirit

1. When we harbor sinful compromises like committing fornication without repentance, yet continue an outward facade of Christianity.

2. When we profess the Christian life but do not bear the fruit of the Spirit which can be summed up in one word: LOVE. This was Carlos' error.

3. When we follow doctrines that diametrically oppose the tenets of Christianity.

4. When we seek spiritual experiences without a balance in the Word and covering of a church.

The religious spirit will generally move on well-intending believers who sincerely love the Lord and hate sin. If the believer soars in the realm of the spirit without proper grounding and church covering, spirits of pride and self-righteousness enter in, deceiving the believer that they are holier than thou. They surpass the activity of the church and the vision of the pastor. Many join the masses of believers who represent the unchurched. This group is hidden away on Sundays, reading their Bible at home, praying at self-constructed altars, taking communion, trying to live independently from the organized Body of Christ.

One dear sister has been out of fellowship from a church for some 15 years after being severely hurt. She has her own sanctuary in her attic with an altar included. There, she holds her own services on Sunday, praying, fasting, and seeking God, but she will not darken the door of a church, not even for a funeral service. The sister is suffering from a spirit of unforgiveness. She has allowed deep hurts to cause her to reject the Body of Christ. Anyone developing a spiritual life independent of the local Body is spiritually sick. Despite how consecrated they are, sickness will prevail.

Biologically, a cell that multiplies independent of the flow of the body becomes cancerous. This is the sad state of not a few of God's people who are disobeying a direct command *"not forsaking the assembly of yourselves together*" (Hebrews 10:25). Many have been repulsed by things that go on in church and retreat to their own Isle of Patmos for safety and sanity, but this is wrong. Others do not want to be under submission to a pastor, deeming themselves far above them spiritually. This is pride. The church, however weak and vacillating, is still the Lord's appointed refuge for every believer. It places necessary boundaries, checks and balances to our spiritual experiences. Remove yourself from the church and you have no covering from this invading host.

There was one brother who'd come to church and testify. His words were forceful and full of truth but his spirit was harsh and condemning. Besides this, he did not know when to sit down and shut up. Churchless himself, he'd comb area assemblies giving his "testimonial preaching" until the building would literally empty. This was the work of a religious spirit; for the fruit of the Holy Spirit is temperance (self-control). If this brother was told to sit down, he became angry and of course, maintained that church was quenching the spirit and putting God in a box. Eventually this brother grew worse and was rejected from nearly every assembly he went to. He had become a lunatic.

Signs of a Lunatic Spirit

1. Extreme independence: When asked what church they belong to, they will commonly reply, "God took me out of denominations," or, "I'm a voice crying out in the wilderness." God will never go against His own Word. The Spirit and the Word must agree. *"Not forsaking yourselves . . ."* (Heb. 10:25).

2. Hypercriticism and judgmentalism especially against the church. Is the church weak? Yes. Is she erring? Yes. Has she been made a public spectacle with the failure of well-known televangelists in recent years? Yes. Is there little difference between the church and the world? Sometimes. She is nonetheless the Lord's Body. He knows how to take care of His Body.

He will get out every spot, wrinkle, and blemish and present her flawless.

3. Outward Christian display (i.e., preaching judgment on street corners, wearing anointing oil on the forehead, refusing to comb one's hair, wearing only certain colors like all white) smacks of a religious demon at work. Though God will take His servants through various measures of discipline, we must take caution. We must discern when it is God, or us, or the enemy. Here is where the covering of sound church leadership and wise counsel comes in. *"In multitude of counsels there is safety"* (Proverbs 24:6).

4. Extreme behavior. One woman said her born-again husband took a hammer and smashed the television screen while declaring that the devil was coming into the house through it. He could have easily unplugged it or changed the programming. Religious spirits love to push people over the edge.

Misuse of Spiritual Gifts

This point cannot be overemphasized. We must never use our spiritual gifts, especially the revelation gifts, to injure, control, blackmail anyone, ever. God never shows us anything for the purpose of destruction. Scores have passed through Deeper Life with exceptional demonstrations of spiritual gifts, but because they did not walk in love, their gifting fell under sway of seducing spirits. I had to dissociate myself from them and pull my sheep from out of the iron-clad jaws. Loving God and His people becomes our haven of protection from these malevolent forces.

Childhood Reminiscence

As a student at Lathrop Elementary, I recall having a new student named Wayne wearing a dingy white shirt, transfer to our third grade class from out of town. Wayne was as peculiar as they come—not merely because he was decidedly unkempt, but because he was a fire and brimestone preacher.

During recess, literally throngs of students and some faculty surrounded him as he boldly proclaimed the scriptures, particularly on the subject of judgment and the wrath of God. When slapped in the face, Wayne would turn the other cheek. When challenged to make it stop snowing, he'd point his finger in the air and make a daring attempt.

What many thought was a new-kid-on-the-block spoof turned out to be dead wrong. Wayne remained intensely consistent in his testimony. He seldom smiled or even spoke for that matter, except when it was time for him to speak about God. I saw Wayne victimized by some very cruel acts, but his peers could not break him. He just was not the typical, frivolous third grader. His no-nonsense demeanor and rigidity eventually won the respect of his peers and they left him alone, accepting him as the childhood preacher.

Besides being a charismatic speaker, Wayne could play a slew of musical instruments. He was also an extraordinary artist. He'd bring his art work, wrinkled and dirty, much like himself, to school to the amazement of all. Additionally, God had given Wayne a brilliant mind.

In fact, twice during our schooling, Wayne was selected to represent the inner city schools in the student state science fair and won first place. During one contest, Wayne entered a detailed poster of the human body with colored veins and arteries intricately intact. The fair shut down as all the judges crowded around Wayne, shooting tough questions at him concerning the human anatomy, questions that medical students would know. Wayne confounded them much like Jesus did the scholars in the temple (Matthew 2:46–47). Although some of the suburban students had literal rockets airborne, they had to give first place title to this little, unkempt, black boy from the ghetto.

Today, some thirty years later, Wayne stalks the streets inebriated, swearing and spitting, sometimes preaching erratically at telephone posts. When he is sober and coherent, you can strike up a decent conversation with him. Even with his wide, toothless grin, paunch belly and bloodshot eyes, there is still a resemblance of that childhood preacher. When he asks for money, I give it to him out of sheer respect for what God had begun in him as a child.

Undoubtedly the call and the anointing were there at an early age. Whatever church Wayne belonged to, they failed to lay this boy upon the altar daily, beseeching God for wisdom and balance. Too often we are thrilled by the gift and the call of the young and forget that there will be journeys in this world that will take tremendous wisdom to get through. Divine wisdom teaches us how to survive in a godless, hostile world and emerge unscathed. Wayne couldn't brave the elements and was engulfed by hordes of demons determined that the work that God had begun in his young life would cease. This is the work of religious demons at their worst. I pray that Wayne gets that opportunity at deliverance that will make the difference in his life.

THE CURIOUS CASE OF THE ARCHBISHOP

During my first year in Canton I sold life and health insurance for a short season, going door to door with very little success. I was just not a sales agent. One day I went to the home of a young woman whom I'd never met before. She had just had her seventh child and lived in a humble dwelling on the Northeast end of town. After my sales pitch she said, "I can tell that you are a saved man." The conversation immediately went upon the Lord and I listened intently as she shared some of her supernatural encounters with God. At one point she said, "I see that you desire to have a perfect heart toward the Lord. But if you want to be a man of faith you have to live the life of faith. You must meet a man in Canton who has already climbed the ladder toward this perfection and faith." She called him an archbishop.

I had yearned to live perfectly before God and still do. The witness of what she said was overpowering. She gave me the name and the address of the man and cautiously, I ventured over after a few days of prayer. When I arrived and beheld him, I was stunned by his striking appearance. He stood tall and lean with flawless skin the color of pure bronze, and eyes that sparkled with undeniable health. I thought that Moses could possibly look like this after forty years in the Midian sun. With a rich and resonating voice he greeted me with a voluminous, "G-G-Glory Hallelujah!" This he did throughout our conversation followed by wide swinging arm gestures.

"I saw you in a vision upon a stage along with other ministers that I shall ordain for the last move of God Revival Center. It is a training center that will be built in Canton where men and women will be prepared for the last day harvest and sent out. God is looking for a people who will let Him have His total way in their lives. G-G-Glory Hallelujah!"

Being young and vulnerable, I pondered in my heart if this was the leading of God and could only concede that it was. I was subsequently ordained a bishop and given my credentials that day for the small fee of one dollar. The license was to be renewed annually so I returned to his house once a year for that purpose. Each visit I learned a little more about the archbishop.

He said that God had turned him into a Jew and he was to keep the Jewish Sabbath at home so church was not a part of his life. Mind you, I was young in the faith and couldn't argue with it because God turned Abram, a Syrian, into a Jew (Romans 4). Who could put it past God? He also said that he was mowing the grass one day and such an anointing fell upon him that he was incapacitated for days. When he sobered up God revealed to him that he had been given the body of a twenty-year-old man. The archbishop was in his mid-seventies at the time and amazingly well preserved. Again, I could not question it. God could do anything.

I nonetheless looked for warning signs, but found none. There was no hint of control or manipulation when he spoke. He never once spoke ill of the Body of Christ, nor slandered anyone. There was a godly persona in word and deed and a deep reverence for God. What impressed me the most was his ability to quote several scripture verses verbatim, indicative of a well-preserved mind. Yet

I kept our relationship at bay, returning only when it was time to get my license renewed.

On one visit, I asked about the building and he responded, "The foundation is laid."

"Where?" I asked.

"I don't know. The people who are constructing it don't even know that they are building a center for the Lord."

My suspicion grew. "How can that be? How can you build a building with certain specifications and use it for another purpose?"

Upon my next visit, he said that God had shown him his wife. She was a single, Jewish girl with an infant son, about fifty years his junior. They would marry soon and have a child. His two children from a previous marriage would be the seed of the flesh and would persecute this new child who was the child of promise as with Ishmael and Isaac. (His children had to be in their mid-forties). Suddenly he dug into his pocket and wrote something down on a crumpled piece of paper.

"That's 2674. The Lord told me to write down each time He has given me a new anointing. He then shows me the anointings on a mantle that I wear in the spirit realm. Upon the mantle are stars. Each star represents a different anointing to do a specific work."

Phew! I was still young in the Lord but not altogether stupid. This was far-fetched. I maintained my composure but grew a bit uneasy. I shot a few questions at him, and he handled them masterfully, but I left convinced of one thing: that I wouldn't return.

Everything came to a head one day when I stumbled upon his name listed in the obituary of the newspaper. The archbishop had died. I went to his house and spoke with surviving sisters and a niece. They were thoroughly disgusted with him. He had been retired for years and no one knew what he did with his money. There wasn't a trace of one check. He was sick and said that the Lord would heal him. He died penniless, and was buried by the state without a funeral, memorial, or headstone.

Saddened by it all, I mourned for days. He was totally deluded. Even his G-G-Glory Hallelujahs were part of the deception of demons. He truly thought it was all God. But who was there to tell him differently? What was the breach? I had missed it on the first visit. He didn't attend church. Church is the safe haven for the spiritual man. It governs our growth, keeps us in balance, and protects us from the invasion of deceiving spirits. Those seeking to grow independent of the church will become spiritually sick. Their visions, dreams, teaching might be abundant, but they will be thrown off track by religious spirits. As flawed as she might be, the church is the city of refuge for the spirit man. It is no wonder that the Hebrews author spoke so plainly:

> "Forsaking not the assembling of yourselves as the manner of some but exhorting one another more as the day approaches." (Hebrews 10:25)

Of course, I repented and destroyed all connecting ties and materials with this delusion. I also renounced my association with him breaking any soul ties that could have formed as a result of our meetings. Yet I did not scorn him. He was a lovely man indeed; sincere, but sincerely deceived—so is everyone who tries to develop a spiritual life independent of the church. Sadly enough, they won't see their own deception. The devil will have them to justify their own errors. It is a horrible pit into which not a few of God's people have fallen into.

I thought about Dr. Farrell. Whenever he moves on to pioneer a new church, he first seeks to be under the authority of a pastor. Although he has a global ministry, he always finds someone to be in submission to. I believe this is the key to his longevity in ministry. We shared the floor at a conference just recently and Dr. Farrell was in rare form. Still anointed, still scriptural, and still balanced. His example is to be applauded.

Chapter 19

THE BABY SPIRIT

Childish fears
Childish hurts
Childish reactions
Pettiness

Childish dependency
Childish traditions
Irresponsibility
Childish behavior

When Erna cried "Mommy, Mommy," I knew that it was merely a tactic of the enemy to stall for time. I later learned that it was the manifestation of what I call the baby spirit. The baby spirit suppresses our natural development into adulthood and maturity. It works against the Holy Spirit's aim for us *"to grow up in all things"* (Eph. 4:15). It is sometimes referred to as arrested development.

After the session, I noticed that Erna did dress like a little girl. Her shoes, hair style and general appearance was neat, but that of an adolescent. God began to show me others who were under the influence of this spirit, particularly at my job.

One of our co-workers was obsessed with holiday traditions. In April, the Easter eggs, bunny rabbits, jelly beans decorations had to be out on display. In November there were harvest pictures, turkey figurines, pumpkins, gourds, etc. In December it was the nativity scene, mistletoe, garlands, ribbons and bows. I even saw him unwrapping a candy bar and placing it in his mouth with a wide sweeping gesture as though an airplane was swooping down into a hangar. At forty years of age, he wore a real Mickey Mouse watch to work faithfully for years. In addition to all this came some of the most juvenile behavior that I've ever witnessed from an adult.

Another worker loved to wear hair barrettes and clothing one could imagine being on a large baby doll. She spoke and behaved much like a child. One day she came up to me declaring gleefully, "Guess what? This weekend I went to three birthday parties, Aimilee my niece's, then Cheryl's, and then we turned around and gave Fred a surprise party." I believe two of the three were children. This was the expression of the baby spirit.

I laughed as I recognized certain behavior that identified this spirit in others, until God took me back into my own life. For years I played an imaginary game as a child. It was similar to taking a pencil and turning it into a train. I would play for hours with this imaginary toy and prefered it over playing with other kids. Adolescence did not break it. The fantasy game followed me right into college. I remember being overjoyed when my roommate didn't show up at Wesleyan. It meant that I had a single room and would have no need to explain my childish behavior. When I went to play with this toy, it struck me. I was in college now preparing to embark upon manhood. It was time to grow up. I put it away and never pulled it out again. My laughter at others was reduced to a hush.

The baby spirit will also manifest in immature emotions. Those under its domain will pout, explode over the least little thing, hurt easily, express unreal levels of selfishness, and reflect the emotional instability of a six-year old. While initially the baby spirit seems harmless, I have seen this spirit operate in more diabolical ways. Childish jealousy, cruelty, vengeance especially in the area of ministry, has shipwrecked divine purposes. People in authority with this spirit will abuse it even as a child would, and this can cause great pain to those who are mature. Marriages have been ruined by one or both partners displaying gross immaturity. This explains why the spirit, like any other spirit, needs to be cast out.

It keeps us from following Paul's exhortation to *"put away childish things"* (I Cor. 13:11). Christianity is a journey along the pathway of personal maturity, endless revelation of God's nature, and a progressive conforming into the image of Jesus. The baby spirit serves to block all three developments.

Playing with your children's toys on Christmas Eve while they lie in bed anticipating the morning is one thing, but acting out as a child in an adult environment is altogether another. This spirit will not only strangle the emotional development of its victim, it will not even allow the person to think maturely, make adult decisions or operate in mature faith. There is an unhealthy co-dependency upon others, for dependency is the nature of a child.

Obsessions with holidays can be one sign of its existence. During Christmas, everything has to be exactly the way it was during our childhood Christmases or our world is rotating backwards. There is an obsession for children's clothes, toys, games, candies, cartoons, comic books, and any child's artifacts. Traditions must be celebrated the same as they were when we were children or we plunge into depression. If someone is not singing happy birthday and bringing us balloons, we are smitten.

To prevent this in our own lives, I told my wife that we would celebrate holidays and birthdays differently. Some years we eat out on holidays and forfeit the big, home-cooked meals. The children may get parties with all the trimmings one year, then we'll have a quiet family session with a gift or two on other birthdays. There may be cake or there may not.

We are not being cruel, but as international ministers, we may be engaged in the Lord's work during special occasions. My son, Josiah, turned one while I was in a conference in Toronto. He also learned to walk there. He and my daughter, Aliena, celebrated their second and first birthdays in England. One year our third child, Nia-Nicole turned three at home in Ohio, while Alva and I ministered on the island of Antigua. To avoid locking them into a tradition and fostering a baby spirit, we keep things different and low key—choosing rather to boost their self-esteem and reaffirm our love for them daily rather than on a particular day.

Chapter 20

ANNIVERSARY SPIRIT

Suicide	Mourning	Grief	Panic Attacks
Sickness	Backsliding	Guilt	Nervous Breakdowns
Depression	Pity Parties	Trauma	Sin Binges

> "To everything there is a season and a time for every purpose under heaven." (Ecc. 3:1)

Solomon says everything has a season. The seasons listed in this beautiful verse in Ecclesiastes have been used in speeches, songs and poems for centuries. The enemy, however, has taken hold of this universal principle and channeled it into a vicious cycle of frustration and defeat through a spirit known as the anniversary spirit.

We first noticed that several people were coming back to deliverance session carrying the same baggage that they had been delivered from, around the same time each year. After prayer and counseling, we came up with the name of the anniversary spirit. It is like a timed release demon that kicks off at a particular season each year.

The cases we saw most repeated were the anniversary backsliding. We could almost time the very day a person would suddenly stop coming to church and end up in a backslidden condition. After months they would return, only to retreat the same time the following year. This was the work of the anniversary spirit. Some literally backslid every time summer approached.

Anniversary suicide was also common among those seeking deliverance. This spirit would link with the spirit of trauma and worthlessness to drive its victim to the point of suicide. Although counseling and befriending a potential suicidal victim is vital in their recovery, we must cast out the spirit of suicide. We have discovered that suicide often stems from a generational curse. Someone on the family tree has attempted suicide and now the spirit fastens itself upon the branch in another generation to carry out the same sad scenario.

Demons cause the victim to look at life with utter despair. When hope is removed, the individual sees no purpose for living. Anything can trigger these flooding feelings: a divorce, financial disaster, taunting and teasing from classroom schoolmates, an unrequited love affair, struggles in the ministry, a business failure, rejection and the overall pressures of life itself. Jesus is not only the light of the world, but the hope of the world also. As long as there is life, there is hope for a better tomorrow. Through the grace of God, we can turn our trials into triumphs, our misery into ministry, and our slip-ups into stepping stones. However, when hope for a brighter tomorrow is washed away, the victim becomes prey to despair and despair opens the door to suicide.

Below is a letter from a dear sister who received not only deliverance, but also an understanding of how the spirit of suicide worked against her. She had failed in many of life's endeavors, shaming the name of her family to the point of rejection, especially from her father. With four out-of-wedlock births from four different fathers she wrote:

"When I can't see any future, no goals, plans—nothing is left to keep me striving—I want to flee from myself. My thoughts are clouded. I tried everything but nothing is working. Then I start to think within myself. This would be the grand finale. To hurt everyone that hurt me. Now they would know my pain. Now they would know how they should have treated a person like me. Now they will find out how much I was truly hurting. This is my chance to get a teardrop, just from them. I will have everyone wishing that they would have only listened to me. Helped me more. Not turned their backs on me. I will get the last response and no one can correct me, for after I commit suicide they will hurt forever, as I have."

—Sharon

Note that one act of suicide can contain the spirit of wounded pride, low self-esteem, rejection, pain, retaliation, vengeance, and attention-getting. The enemy's greatest weapon is to get us to turn inward and evaluate ourselves from the perspective of self-worth, and not from God's righteousness. When everything comes up worthless, we lose our purpose to live. We inhale blackness. Death becomes a welcome relief. Satisfaction is gained in knowing that we have issued the ultimate payback to those who have hurt or rejected us. This is the sickness of suicide.

No single event or season defines our destiny, only God does. No single act defines our end: not tragedy, rejection, setbacks, sins, failures, layoffs, divorce. We have every reason to persevere and see a turnaround. God takes the foolish things and weak things of the earth to confound the wise and mighty.

When treating a suicidal person it goes beyond merely casting out a devil. You must be a parent or best friend to the person, if possible. Most suicide comes from being faced with pressures that cause the person to turn inward. They have nothing to pull from, because they are depleted of hope. Their tomorrow is forlorn and their future is black—just like their soul. They cannot see God who is our Hope for tomorrow. Some steps in dealing with potential suicide victims are:

1. Bind the spirit of suicide, hopelessness and despair (silently if need be).

2. Reject any stroll down pity party alley. Speak hope, confidence in a tomorrow, and the possibilities of change in the present circumstance.
3. Encourage the person to eat a hearty meal, get the blood sugar level increased.
4. Change the environment. Go to a park, the mountains, the beach. Let the beauty of nature minister to the individual.
5. Point the person toward God's infinite love and acceptance.
6. Look for someone for the person to help. Rake leaves, shovel snow, help someone move, wash a car—as we take the focus off of our wounded selves and place it on others' needs, we slowly develop a sense of worth and purpose.
7. Stay with the individual as long as possible. You may have to solicit help.

Ashley's Case

Ashley had been molested throughout her childhood by three men, one of whom used a knife. He carved tiny slits on her chest as a warning of what awaited her if she told anyone. She then was about nine years old. As an adult, Ashley had bouts of severe depression that made her suicidal. She'd use a knife to make cuts in her childhood scars. We worked hard and long to dislodge this spirit along with many others related to rape. She is walking in her deliverance and now leads a productive and prosperous Christian life.

Anniversary Adultery

I ministered to one brother, a minister, who committed adultery on a seasonal basis. No matter how well his marriage was going, or how satisfactory his marriage bed was, he found himself plowing in a field that was not his. I made it clear that the spirit of adultery is never satisfied until it has caused its victim to cheat or rob the affections of a married person. I had one Christian sister say, "Toni, I won't even give a man a second look unless he's married." This was the spirit of adultery speaking. This sister had already broken up one marriage and the spirit gloated over the thought of being able to take a man from his wife. She was in need of some serious deliverance in spite of being a wonderful person otherwise.

Whenever we are caught in a web of moral sins, we must get to the root of the problem. A background check is usually necessary. However painful, honesty helps us judge the level of bondage, identify and dislodge the spirits that have entered in. Next, it will take renouncing the sin and the people we have been involved with. We must see the sin as God sees it. Then we must walk free, resisting every temptation to return.

Another culprit is anniversary sin binges. The believer just goes wild in sin, often drinking and carousing for a weekend before crashing into a deep despair. Confession and repentance follow, until the next bout. Many say, "I don't know why I keep doing this!" It is the work of the anniversary spirit. We have cast out anniversary depression, nervous breakdown, and sickness, with some remarkable results.

Anniversary Mourning

Anniversary mourning is a most difficult spirit to overcome because of what life means to us as human beings. A mother's grief runs deeper than anyone else's because she knew the child from the time that she was aware of her pregnancy. Men also are not exempt from deep mourning over the loss of someone, especially a son or daughter.

> "And the king was much moved, and went up to the chamber over the gate, and wept; and as he went, thus he said, O my son Absalom, my son, my son Absalom! Would God I had died for thee, O Absalom, my son, my son!" (II Samuel 18:33)

> "And he knew it, and said, It is my son's coat; an evil beast hath devoured him; Joseph is without doubt rent in pieces. And Jacob

rent his clothes, and put sack cloth upon his loins, and mourned for his son many days." (Genesis 37:33–34)

David and Jacob are featured in the above scriptures as fathers deeply grieved by the their sons' deaths. David never recovered from the death of Absalom. Jacob of course, had a happier ending, yet grief nearly broke his heart. There are no simple answers or instructions on grieving. The key is that we must mourn then go through it. Life is a vapor. We are born to fulfill our purpose, then we go on home. Should a little one pass on to be with the Lord, it means that purpose, for whatever reason, was cut short. But we must go on. David gave the proper response when he lost his first son with Bathsheba. *"I shall go to him, but he shall not return to me"* (2 Samuel 12:23).

It is said that Jesus comes for the little ones. We know that they are in the best of hands. When a child is taken, it is certain that they had to be very special to Him. We can never be angry with God, because all souls are His. We do not own one thing, including our children. The scriptures make it clear that they are God's heritage. Therefore when loved ones are taken away from us, whether by God or the enemy, prematurely or on God's timetable, we thank God for the time He's blessed us with their presence and we move on, knowing that death is merely a conclusion of the temporal life into an eternal one.

In the Old Testament there was a specific time for mourning. Israel mourned for Aaron thirty days (Num. 20:29) and the Egyptians for Jacob seventy (Gen. 50:3), and then they moved on. We must do the same. Although grief can never be put on a timetable, we must mourn then press our way on lest the anniversary spirit begin to make our grief perpetual.

Chapter 21

ANGER

Vengeance	Past Memories	Hatred for pastors
Rage	Wrath	Violence
Hatred for men	Assault	Hatred for gays
Hatred for women	Militarism	Rooted Bitterness

The spirit of anger is directly related and linked to the spirit of unforgiveness. Forgiveness is a grace from God. As it is with love, forgiveness is a part of our salvation package. It must be developed and exercised throughout life if we are to see and demonstrate its beauty.

When we fail to forgive—that is, to let go; to loose; to pardon an offense; to cancel a debt, a wrong done; we fall into a major pit and allow the spirit of anger to become a perpetual torment to us. God emphasized this point in a marvelous parable in Matthew 18.

God taught me several things about this because I suffered from unforgiveness as a child. I just couldn't let go of a wrong. I would retain it for days on end and it would alter my entire personality. I always wanted to be nice, but forces kept me bitter and combative.

For example, if a rainy day canceled recess everyone could adjust but me. I'd pout and stomp, refusing to work to my fullest potential for the balance of the day. I can remember my second grade teacher, Ms. Calhoun, wrote on my report card, "Toni becomes hurt when things do not go his way. If he does not mature, it will hurt his grades because he has a temper!" I was mad at those comments for days!

The point is true. Demons keep us from maturing and developing emotionally as God intended. There are scores of forty-year-old men behaving like six-year-olds because of the spirit of anger. What is sadder still, the spirit of anger opens the door to more dangerous spirits like violence and murder.

During sibling arguments, I was the one who raced to the kitchen drawer to get the butcher knife. At seven years old, this was an extreme. It is only by the grace of God that we didn't have a tragedy. I'd wake up in the morning burning mad because I lost at a game of ping pong the night before. The rest of my day was ruined by a negative attitude. Ephesians has some vital tips in dealing with the spirit of anger. *"Be ye angry, and sin not; let not the sun go down upon your wrath"* (4:26). After this command we get another, *"neither give place to the devil"* (4:27). Satan operates on the ground of unresolved anger. In fact, no emotions will express his nature more than the emotion of anger. Believers beware. Our anger should be directed toward unrighteousness; it should be a holy anger. Those who blow up over the least little thing are probably under the oppression of this spirit and need deliverance.

Forgiveness is the antidote to the spirit of anger. I've taught seminars on the stronghold of unforgiveness. The word stronghold means a fortress whereby something is kept safely within; impenetrable wall of protection. There are good strongholds, and of course, bad strongholds. In bad strongholds, demon forces are kept behind the walls of our heart and we are tormented by them. These are some areas of forgiveness that must be covered if we are to walk in victory. You must:

1. Instantly forgive those who have hurt you.
2. Forgive the past: past events, past traumas, unexplained tragedies.
3. Forgive places where bad things occurred.

4. Forgive the day, the hour, the second, the moment.
5. Forgive yourself.
6. Forgive God.

Let's deal with each individually, because each plays a different role in dismantling the stronghold of unforgiveness.

Forgiving people

A book could be written on this subject alone, especially if you are in the ministry. Jesus said, *"offenses come,"* (Matt. 18:7). This speaks of the many contrary words and attitudes levied against us as we do the Lord's work. We must forgive them lest we become a gall of bitterness. God forgave us of much worse.

Forgiving the past

Rehearsing past hurts and bitterness will put you in a pit of despair. The enemy will box you in and you will become introspective. Once we turn inward, darkness floods the soul and we become blind to the hope that is in God. In this state, any negative thing can happen. We become poisoned by circumstances that God wants us to use as stepping stones into maturity. Unforgiveness stunts our growth, and is the major crippler in Christianity.

Forgiving places

One day I had a chance to go back to the Wesleyan campus. I reacted violently inside. I had not let go of the negativism. We must learn to release the places where we have had bad experiences. Had Jesus held a grudge against Samaria when the city rejected Him and called down fire from heaven as the sons of thunder suggested, Phillip would have never brought such marvelous revival there, recorded in the Book of Acts. We must let go of places.

Forgiving the day

We will always have good days and challenging days. Then there are days when we face fierce trials and sometimes tragedy. David helps us face our days by declaring, *"This is the day that the*

Lord hath made; we will rejoice and be glad in it" (Ps. 118:24). Every day is permeated with God's goodness. He comes as the Teacher, the Comforter, the Hero, the Discipliner. He is always there to guide us into a higher creativity of resolving problems. It produces a greater level of existence. Therefore, the day is always good.

Forgiving ourselves

We will experience many setbacks and failures in the area of sin, which will never surprise God, because He clearly knows our end from our beginning. It will, however, surprise us. Some of the things we will do along this journey will be shocking, but we must forgive ourselves and press on. This is not justification of a wrong. We are justified by His grace whereby we have peace with God. Now walk in that peace. Walk in the forgiveness of God, and put no confidence in the flesh.

Forgiving God

Yes, we must even forgive God at times. Please understand this truth—there is no fault in God, ever (Proverbs 21:30). He is absolutely righteous and unswervingly good (James 1:17). Yet throughout our Christian walk we will pass through much sorrow and many hot trials. Should God offer us no explanation, we need to loose Him from any indebtedness.

As a counselor, I've been bombarded by questions such as, "Why did God let my grandmother die?" "Why did He let this happen?" "Why did He let that happen?" "He could have prevented it."

Without an answer to their questions or a quick remedy to their immaturity, I've simply implored them to release God (forgiveness in its rawest form), work through the anger and the pain, and go on loving Him.

Chapter 22

WITCHCRAFT

Ouija Board	Fortune Telling	Spiritualism
Seance	Astrology	Superstition
Tarot Card	Palm Readings	Divination
New Age Philosophy	Eastern Religions	Psychic Friends Hotline

MADISON

Madison came to our Saturday evening deliverance service seeking help. She had lost nearly everything she owned due to mental illness. Medicine kept her stable, but she was still plagued with haunting thoughts and hallucinations. When we went to pray for her, I felt that force again. I had to back off. Only one other worker felt it. We asked if there had been occult involvement and she said yes. We worked with her for nearly an hour with little results. This force acted as a shield against our words. Even her repentance was blocked. There was no brokenness, no real conviction for sin. She just sat there listlessly, repeating the sinner's prayer. Surely the power of God is greater than the power of the enemy. But it is only effective on a broken and contrite heart.

I don't believe Madison received much help. Darkness held a strong grip upon her. We sent her away believing that God would yet work in due season. The moral of the lesson, I told the deliverance team, is that witchcraft of all sorts, is to be shunned as a plague. Don't even allow the psychics to enter your family room from the television with their damnable divination.

Shana

I was visiting a friend in Detroit when his wife began to share some strange occurences in the household. Apparently their six-year-old son had a toy car with a remote and the car was moving without the power of the remote control. Other strange things were happening in the house. Shana, their teenage daughter, and her brother both saw shadows in the house on a regular basis. The boy spent many frightened nights in bed with his parents. I gathered everyone to the dining room table and began an interview, but I felt led to focus on Shana. She was as sweet as they come, so I gently began to ask her some questions.

"Shana, I'm going to ask you some personal questions. I need you to answer them as honestly as you can. Do you have any girl friends?"

"Yes," she said.

"Have you ever spent the night over at any of their homes?" I asked

"Yes, at Connie's."

"How many times?" I asked.

"Twice."

"What did you do?"

"We played, ate, talked about school . . . that kind of stuff," she answered.

"Did you ever play with an Ouija board while you were there?"

Shana looked a little confused, so I described the board with its various numbers and letters.

"Yes, we played with one," she said.

"What did you ask the board?"

"We asked it about what the weather would be and if Ken liked Olivia."

"Did you play with this only once?"

"Yes."

At that, I lectured the entire family on the evils of dabbling in the occult. They were experiencing demon invasion called *poltergeist*, a German word for spirit knocking. Demons began to actively engage in the natural realm with noises, appearances, and destructive behavior. When the toy was mentioned as running on its own, I knew that a door had been opened to the spirit world through a violation. This was a godly home with both parents active in ministry. I surmised it was coming from an outside source, so I interviewed Shana.

We held hands and went into a prayer of repentance. We renounced all involvement in the occult. I then bound the spirit of divination and witchcraft and commanded it to leave. I closed the door in the spirit realm and covered the entire house and family with the blood. I prayed for Connie and her family that they would see the evil of this game and remove it immediately. To my knowledge the family was plagued no more.

I remember one autumn, a young lady came to the church from a battered women's shelter. She was in a quandary of whether to leave her husband or give the relationship another try. We led her to the Lord and placed the issue in the Lord's hand. Whenever I gazed into her eyes, I had the strangest feeling of discomfort. I did not get the witness until she walked into the church wearing a jersey with a black cat and cauldron. It was the Halloween season, but this was no excuse. The power emanating from her eyes had intensified.

After prayer I called her aside and asked her if she had engaged in any occult experiences. It was very difficult to look her in the face. I rattled off some common occult experiences and she admitted calling the Psychic Friend's Network.

"How often," I asked.

"Several times a day, sometimes," she replied.

"Why?"

"I need to know what to do about my husband. Should I leave him or what?"

I ended up giving her a lecture on the dangers of the occult and then went into deliverance after she repented. Sad to say, we got no results. That Sunday, the influence was still there. Months later, I received a call from her and she again was asking should she leave her husband, who was a legal alien. She believed he married her for a "green card" and needed direction. In the same statement she mentioned calling the psychics again. I was upset. It was nearly one in the morning and I hadn't seen her in church for weeks and now this.

Her case is that of many. The psychic telephone hot lines get millions of dollars from God's people who are looking for answers that could easily be obtained through the Bible and from sitting under sound Word ministries. One thing for sure, God is no hotel bellhop. He does not cater to our cries of impatience. Waiting upon the Lord is an unalterable principle of the kingdom. *"Wait upon the Lord; be of good courage, and he shall strengthen thine heart. Wait, I say, on the Lord"* (Ps. 27:14). Today, many of God's people are crossing over into witchcraft by dabbling in the occult without the slightest idea of its dire consequence. It is time for the church to rise up in knowledge and teach the unadulterated Word of the Most High God.

Chapter 23

THE CURSED WOMAN: JEZEBEL

The key to understanding Jezebel is found in Revelation 2. It is the Lord's rebuke to the church of Thyatira. When I read it, the Holy Spirit had me highlight certain words which would give a clear profile of Jezebel. Since it is a major principality over the Canton area and will have predominance in the end times, it is necessary that we glean all we can concerning this wicked spirit.

> "And unto the angel of the church in Thyatira write: These things saith the Son of God, who hath his eyes like a flame of fire, and his feet are like fine brass. I know thy works, and charity . . . Notwithstanding, I have a few things against thee, because thou **sufferest that woman**, Jezebel, who **calleth herself** a prophetess, **to teach** and to seduce my servants to commit fornication, and to eat things sacrificed unto idols. And I gave her space to repent of her fornication, and **she repented not**. Behold, I will cast her into a bed, and them that commit adultery with her into great tribulation, except they repent of their deeds. And I will kill **her children** with death; and all the churches shall know that I am he who **searcheth the reins and hearts**; and I will give unto every one of you according to your works. But unto you I say, and unto the rest in Thyatira, as many as have not this doctrine, and who have not known the depths of Satan, as they

speak, I will put upon you no other burden. But that which ye have already, hold fast till I come."

In Thyatira, Jezebel was allowed to teach false doctrine to the congregation. In my first encounter with Jezebel, the individual taught Tuesday night Bible study. Not only was there no anointing, but she began to subtly inject poisonous opposition toward me and the church vision. As the warfare intensified, her intentions became blatant. One night she taught from II Kings 7, concerning the four lepers. Her last words were, "We can either sit here and die or you can follow me."

No one was about to follow her to hell, I thought to myself, but inner thoughts were unacceptable to God. I was allowing this poisoning to take place (thou sufferest). Jezebel's teaching was full of leaven—pastor, you cannot allow Jezebel to weave her ensnaring web over your flock. Jezebel will seek a position of authority whereby she may secretly rule. It will frequently be a teaching post. If given the chance, she will turn every living soul against you and the vision of the church through witchcraft. Throw her down!

The next trait deals with her self-appointment into the prophetic office: she calls *"herself a prophetess."* Herein lies a note of caution for all women used in the prophetical calling and who operate in the revelation gifts. Whenever your revelations are coming against headship, the church elders, or doctrine, it is time to examine your source. If such revelations are causing you to despise headship, you are under the influence of Jezebel. If you are now spreading these revelations to other members of the Body, you are seducing them into your own delusion. You are cloning.

A clone is an imitation of a thing from which it is derived. It is a copy. It is through Jezebel's whispering divination that her victims are cloned and begin to act out her rebellion. They become *"her children"* in verse 23. We also call them eunuchs. Generally, Jezebel will stay camouflaged while her clones (offspring) do all the ranting, criticizing, challenging and rebelling based upon her revelations on what is or isn't going on in the church.

In verse 21, God gives Jezebel space to repent but she doesn't. Herein lies the danger of the Jezebellian principality. It will not allow its victim to feel godly sorrow. She will not see her wrong from God's perspective, for it is godly sorrow that works toward repentance (II Corinthians 7:10). Before she will admit her wrong and submit to authority, she will leave the congregation, ripping up the very carpet on her way out if possible. Though she leaves the church, she will not repent, neither will her clones unless they are delivered. The Lord then took me to Revelation, Chapter 9 which deals with the seven trumpet judgments.

> "And the rest of the men who were not killed by these plagues yet **repented not** of the works of their hands, they should not worship devils and idols of gold, and silver, and brass, and stone, and wood, which neither can see, nor hear walk. **Neither repented** they of their murders, nor of their sorceries, nor of their fornication, nor of their thefts . . . And men were scorched with great heat, and blasphemed the name of God, who hath power over these plagues; and they **repented not** to give him glory. . . . And [they] blasphemed the God of heaven because of their pains and their sores, and **repented not** of their deeds." (Revelations 9:20–21; 16:9,11)

> "And I gave her space to repent . . . and she **repented not**." (Revelation 2:21)

Comparing the two texts in Revelation, we see that Jezebel is a reigning principality in the end time, causing men to "repent not" though they clearly know that it is God who's judging them. Jezebel hardens the hearts of men beyond repentance, making her one of the most ominous forces in our generation. This is why we must step up a fierce defense against her wickedness. This is why we must throw her down lest she cast us into a bed of hell.

The Lord introduces Himself as the Son of God, *"who searcheth the reins and hearts."* For years in the pastorate I had combatted Jezebel manifesting herself through women undermining my ministry, but not until I read *The Three Battlefields* by Francis

Frangipane, did I see Jezebel in an even deeper light. As we said, she is behind sexual impurity, for she literally *"seduces my servant to commit fornication."* Frangipane depicted Jezebel coming in the form of sexual indiscretions, like the onslaught of adultery and pornography currently running rampant in the church. He makes it clear that we cannot despise her operating in the church and then entertain her in our bedroom VCR and on the Internet during late night hours.

Currently hordes of believers are ensnared by the stronghold of pornography and sexual impurity of all sorts. It is the despicable work of Jezebel. She wins no matter how well we preach or how large our congregations are. She prevails in the heart through our unholy compromises. We become no different than her palace eunuchs.

New York

Back in 1992, God sent me to New York on an unforgettable mission. I was invited to speak for a pastor friend who was renovating an abandoned car garage into a thousand-seat sanctuary. As we toured the premises, he explained how the garage floor contained foot-deep crud that was hauled away along with tires, generators, batteries, oil and scrap metal. The platform, musicians quarter, offices, sound room were all framed in grandiose style. Thousands of dollars had been pumped into the vision with several thousands needed for its completion. Membership was racing toward a mega church level. The vision was huge and breathtakingly impressive.

Before leaving home, God spoke prophetically that He was going to deal with some issues in New York. No stone would go unturned. He told me not to hold back and that New York was going to know that He was God! I was apprehensive, of course, but committed to do God's will.

Accompanied by a van load from Canton, I was prepared to teach a three-part session on rebellion and the spirit of Jezebel, a subject that I was quite familiar with. Friday night went as planned but Saturday night's teaching was preempted by an anointing that I could scarcely stand up under. Through the gift of prophecy God pronounced judgment on the entire church, saying that the lifestyles of His people exceeded the filth that was once on the garage floor. He said that this church would receive His "highest and most severe judgment."

At one point, I was moved to speak directly to one of the young ministers, warning him about the consequences of his actions (which were not revealed). God also moved out on the pastor and told him that He had some things to speak to him in private.

When the anointing lifted, I didn't know what to say. You could hear a feather drop. When an altar call was made, the entire church came forward! The pastor wandered nervously throughout the hundred or so at the altar. I knew nothing about mass deliverance at that time, so I laid my hands on a few folks, then told the rest to stay if they felt a need to do so.

After Sunday's message, Erna and I privately counseled the twenty-three-year-old minister who confessed to having sexual relations with one of the church sisters for more than two years. He also had an addiction to pornography which he had indulged in the very night God spoke to him. There was not a day that went by where he didn't have at least one pornographic fantasy.

After a brief sexual history, I hastily called out the spirits. Suddenly we heard a low voice say, "We'll come out for now."

After some prodding, I was able to cast out three powerful spirits named lust, fantasy lust and pornography. They departed with a force that hurled him backwards. I advised him to speak to his pastor about his problem and he consented.

As we finished, it was announced that my flight time was near. We sped dangerously through traffic only to miss my flight. After calling home to make arrangements for an extended vacation, I returned to the pastor's home. The pastor remained aloof my entire stay; therefore, no personal ministry took place. This disturbed me because I did not want to be held accountable for an unfinished assignment. Nonetheless, I was never so glad to board a plane home. That next morning I received an early call from Marie, one of our intercessors.

"Pastor, I've been crying and interceding all morning for the church in New York. They let that sensual spirit get into the congregation, pastor. God is so grieved."

"Uh, huh," I confirmed and said nothing more.

It was several weeks before I spoke to the pastor.

"Pastor, there's some terrible problems with your people," I said with great brokenness.

"I know, I talked with my minister. Some others had confessions to make to me after you left," he said.

"Pastor, you have some good teachers within the congregation. You need to set them up to teach the people about the holiness of God . . ."

"It's none of my business what the people do after service. That's between them and God!" he snapped.

I could scarcely believe what had been said. I was not about to argue. The conversation ended on a sorrowful note. He did thank me for coming and appeared to hold no grudges as to what happened. This was no solace, however. God was grieved. *"Righteousness exalteth a nation but sin is a reproach to any people"* (Proverbs 14:34). Some months later he called asking for prayer. Within a matter of days the Fire Marshall was coming to padlock the church. I received a letter from his associate, informing me that he and his family had left. The Fire Marshall came with the padlock to close the church up while the pastor and a handful of people were praying fervently before God. The rest of the flock had scattered.

Later, the pastor called to inform me of his reorganizing efforts. The former ministry no longer existed. A new name and government had been drafted. He had lost all but a faithful few and was sharing a building with another ministry. My head was spinning.

I realized that Jezebel was in the church, but not as I depicted her in my teaching. She had come against the "reins and the heart" of the congregation. They had been seduced into fornication and repented not, hence the work folded.

Eventually, I understood what God's highest and most severe judgment was. It occurs when God blots out the name of a people, place or thing from under heaven. Whenever God wipes a thing off His slate in heaven it will become a byword here on earth. It no longer represents Him or it has come against divine purpose, therefore He makes it extinct. The thing has reached an apex of God's divine indignation.

This happened in Exodus, Chapter 17, when the Amalekites withstood Israel in the wilderness. They touched the very heart of God. Covenant was being violated. God's offense was irreparable. He spoke to Moses, *"Write this for a memorial in a book, and rehearse it in the ears of Joshua; for I will utterly put out the remembrance of Amalek from under heaven"* (Exodus 17:14). This is God's severest judgment on earth. It happened to PTL; it could happen to any one of us. Let us walk softly before His holiness. Let us wage a fervent war against Jezebel. Let us pray like the great psalmist, *"Lord, my heart is not haughty, nor mine eyes lofty; neither do I exercise myself in great matters, or in things too high for me"* (Psalm 131:1).

Hatred

In Mark 6:14–27, we see something amazing occurring in the spirit realm. Salome, the stepdaughter of Herod, had just finished her salacious dance. The King's blood pressure was up, his brow sweating and mouth salivating. He hastily granted her a blank check, up to half the kingdom. The poor girl was only a teenager. Having not a clue of what she might ask, she turned to her mother, Herodias.

Now what would your response be if this had been your daughter? Would you ask for half the kingdom? A full ride to Harvard? A million dollars? The best looking man in Israel? What did Herodias request? The head of John the Baptist. As we said, John came in the Spirit of Elijah, which means that he operated under the same anointing. Their consecration was similar. Their zeal, dress, social isolation all resembled one another. If the anointing of Elijah was in Jerusalem at this time, guess whose spirit was there to challenge it? You guessed correctly: Jezebel. Jezebel was operating in Herodias. Of all the things a mother could want for her daughter, Herodias requested the death of John, who had publically rebuked her illicit marriage.

Hope for Jezebel

I do not want to sound fatalistic. God wants those who have fallen prey to Jezebel to repent and become a part of the Body flow once again. There must be deep repentance and acknowledgment of one's wrong in respect to authority. Here are some scriptural steps:

> "'Only acknowledge thy sins . . .'" (Jeremiah 3:13)

> 'Seek ye the Lord while He may be found, call ye upon him while he is near; let the wicked forsake his way and the unrighteous man his thoughts, and let him return unto the Lord, and he will have mercy upon him; and to our God, for he will abundantly pardon." (Isaiah 55:7)

1. Acknowledge that Jezebel has been using you to damage the Body, headship at home and/or church.
2. Renounce her influence upon you. This may take verbal, open confession and intense prayer.
3. Go to those in authority (husband, pastors, elders) you have defied and apologize. The root of pride, deceit and denial must be cut by the spirit of humility.
4. Loose every clone or eunuch that has been a part of your damning entourage. Separate yourself from them if necessary.
5. Reacquaint yourself with God. The spirit of Jezebel blinds us from a true relationship with God's holiness, respect for authority, and submission.
6. Learn all you can about this principality and take instant authority over it the moment it begins to manifest itself. Go into

a sustained warfare for your soul, praying in the spirit as often as possible.

7. Submit yourself to authority. Position yourself scripturally to your husband, allowing him to lead. Become an armor bearer for your pastor. Ask God to give you an undying love for him or her. Become a watchman for the church. As a former captive you will readily identify the traits and characteristics of Jezebel. Become a traitor to this principality. Whenever you see her in operation, throw her down.

8. Those men caught in the web of adultery and pornography must follow the same procedure by renouncing these sins and dissolving every tie to them. Do not take it lightly. Just recently a stranger asked for a ride from two teen girls leaving a video store and savagely raped and killed one, leaving the other for dead in the Dover, Ohio area. The survivor was able to identify the assailant. It was a young father of three. His wife said that her husband was under the influence of violent music and pornography on the Internet. These forces had opened the door to the spirit of rape, violence and murder.

Chapter 24

THE KORAH / ABSALOM SPIRIT

Korah represents the male counterpart to Jezebel. Whereas Jezebel's insect type is a black widow, Korah is a scorpion. Both have deadly stings. In dealing with the spirit of rebellion, a leader must not only keep an eye on the principle of Jezebel which operates primarily through the sisters, but he must also keep a close eye on the activity of the brothers as well. For there will always be someone in the congregation who thinks that he can run the church better than the pastor, preach and teach better, love more fervently, etc. Here are some of the words spoken from those who may be under the influence of the Korah spirit:

"Let's pray that the pastor gets a stronger revelation in the Word."

"Uh, I'm not sure about the vision the pastor has, maybe we should meet."

"He's not using the men in the congregation. We have ministries too. He wants the spotlight."

As a descendant of Levi, Jacob's third son, Korah was granted special duties pertaining to the tabernacle worship, but this wasn't enough. Korah wanted that which only Aaron's descendants were privileged to—the priesthood (Num. 16:8–10). After seducing the 250 renowned men famous in the congregation, Korah confronted the unsuspecting Moses with allegations that were clearly false. Fueled by the spirit of envy, Korah took his complaints to leaders of the congregation before ever appearing before Moses. Already his ulterior motive was exposed, for Korah did not want a resolution to the problem—but a revolution. His revolt was not against Moses, but God. We can never attack delegated authority without touching God. The church must hear this message and heed.

Through the power of suggestion (witchcraft), Korah convinced the entire congregation that Moses was guilty of self exaltation. Moses was holding the rest of the leaders down by overextending himself because he didn't want to share the limelight or the power. The charges were absurd. Moses was the meekest man on the planet earth. His Body consciousness was astute. *"And Moses said unto him, enviest thou for my sake? Would God that all the Lord's people were prophets, and that the Lord would put his Spirit upon them"* (Numbers 11:29)! A meek spirit does not retaliate at the injustices of others. Moses fell on his face. This would be a battle that God would fight for him.

Since it was power that they wanted, Moses told them to take censers and light them. Tomorrow God would show who were approved and who were not. Moses then prayed that God would not accept their offering. The censers were bowls which contained incense that burned in the inner court of the tabernacle. It represented the perpetual prayers of the saints. Only the Aaronic priesthood held this distinguished privilege. The moment these princes took censers from the altar of incense they became the false prophets of the altar. They were ministering in an area where they were never called. This is most serious.

Levi had the distinct honor of handling the artifacts of the tabernacle and the tent itself; nevertheless, this was not enough. They wanted to serve God in a more sacred capacity. *"And no man taketh this honor upon himself, but he that is called of God, as was Aaron"* (Hebrews 5:4). The men had committed the iniquity of the priesthood. They touched that which was reserved for a selected few.

What this means to us in the New Testament era is significant. We cannot tread in territory that we have not been called into by the Divine. Neither can we operate in an anointing nor a calling that God has never ordained. Man can lay hands on us and license us, but if God does not sanction our call or work, we are simply false. Calling yourself a prophet when God has not said so is serious. It is the same with calling oneself an evangelist, pastor or any of the fivefold ministries. Currently, there is a Bishop and Apostle craze going on in the Body. Everyone is clamoring for titles. Many want to serve God but cannot wait on their ministries. Others simply want to do that which God has not anointed them to do. At any rate, if they are not corrected, they will make up the hordes of false ministers, who will challenge God's true anointed in the last days.

Korah was crafty, confrontational and charismatic. When he spoke, the spirit of seduction swept the congregation. They believed his words over Moses' character and leadership. It is unbelievable how rebellion blinds its victim. This blindness is the power of witchcraft (I Samuel 15:23). Rebellion zaps its victim in a mesmerizing trance and then snowballs into a rapid cloning. One open gate: the eye gate, ear gate, mouth gate, that is not governed by the Word of God, can sweep an individual into a tide of subversion. This sweeping rebellion happened again when the ten spies brought back a negative report on Canaan. Everyone who hopes to stand faithful in a congregation with a vision, must guard what they hear, see and speak.

We had a Korah emerge in our midst through a brother who initially came in being a tremendous blessing to me and the ministry but he fell sway to the spirit of rebellion. He became so deluded that at one point he came walking down the aisle during testimony service, ranting and challenging the ministry. He was drowned out with praises. That was before we established divine order. If he would try such a thing now, he would find himself dumped outside in the parking lot by the watchmen who are assigned to protect headship.

Moses' response was not typical. Such spirit emerged from a broken and contriteness which only comes through years of discipline. Moses handled it well, but deep inside we know he was hurt.

Hurt, because the people whom he was called to lead were constantly challenging his authority and misunderstanding his character. Countless pastors are hurt regularly by parishioners who won't connect with the church vision but seek to establish their own. When corrected, they are offended, lift up their heels and leave, taking with them the pastor's virtue.

At one point in pastoring, I thought my very heart would break and my very head would snap. I felt as though the ministry in Canton was an emotional rape where pastors are chewed and spat out after all the flavor was gone. I didn't understand why I felt so deeply in despair until I heard a message entitled, "Keepers of the Flame," preached by Bishop T.D. Jakes. The text was taken from II Samuel 21:15–17:

> "Moreover, the Philistines had yet war again with Israel; and David went down, and his servants with him, and fought against the Philistines. And David waxed faint. And Ishbibenob, who was of the sons of the giant, the weight of whose spear weighed three hundred shekels of brass in weight, he being girded with a new sword, thought to have slain David. But Abishai, the son of Zeruiah, succoured him, and smote the Philistine, and killed him. Then the men of David sware unto him, saying, Thou shalt go no more out with us to battle, that thou quench not the light of Israel."

David was trying to do something in his latter years that he could easily do in his youth: slay giants. But age and war had taken their toll on the King, and David was almost wiped out by a Philistine giant. David's men rescued him, and retired him from battle altogether. They referred to David as the light of Israel. Why should it be threatened, blown out? They could deal with the giants themselves. After all, they have supped from his table, followed his wise counsel, reaped the benefits of a blessed ministry, waxed valiant in fight through his example and training. It was time for them to pour back into his life and ministry, as he had poured into theirs, lest he would faint.

I realized that as scores of people had marched through Deeper Life receiving hours of training, counseling, deliverance, teaching, compassion, fellowship, concern, etc., very few remained to help establish the vision. This will make the heart of any pastor faint. The word faint means to give up, to quit out of exasperation. The law of reciprocity is broken. If we withdraw from our bank accounts without regular deposits, our accounts will bear non-sufficient funds. We must give back to those who have given our new start in life. We cannot muzzle the ox that treads out the corn.

Many times I felt so worthless that I wanted to disintegrate and become a non-existing entity. All this was due to the lack of people who would be keepers of the flame, those who would help me bear the burden of ministry. It goes beyond an encouraging word, "that was a good message, pastor." It is being there; it's punctuality, holding your post, dependability, fruit-bearing, trustworthiness, defending headship, meeting needs, dealing with petty issues between the parishioners and being there for pastors as they were there for you.

Pastors need keepers of the flame; those who will stand with them even as they make their mistakes while growing in the Lord. If all we come to church to do is to pull from headship and suck up the anointing and Word without giving back in full support of the vision, it becomes a type of spiritual vampirism.

At one point in Canton, a relatively small city, there were some 18 or more churches without pastors in both the black and white community, not including those missing from other communities. I knew some of these men personally. Very few left the ministry because of moral or financial controversy. Most left because they could not fulfill their vision within. The opposition, obstinance and rebellion from the people whom they led proved to be too much. Some churches ended on the front page of our local newspaper, *The Repository*, in court. The judge had to remind God's people that church matters belonged in a church forum. How embarrassing. Others left because they did not have keepers of the flame, men and women who would undergird and protect them from the onslaught of the enemy. Many left broken-hearted.

One might say, "I haven't joined in any rebellion against headship, I haven't done anything." That is the problem: you've done nothing. Church is not a drive-in movie where we sit down for two hours to be entertained. Every member must be actively engaged in the vision of the church, supplying that which is lacking, according to their gifting and talents. Then the church will swell to full capacity because God will see that His people have finally come to the knowledge of spiritual service. We are saved to serve, not saved to sit.

The Absalom Spirit

Whereas Korah is bold and brazen in his rebellion, Absalom is subtle, more cunning in his ploy to rally members against headship. His animal type is a serpent.

> "And Absalom rose up early, and stood beside the way of the gate; and it was that, when any man who had a controversy came to the king for judgment, then Absalom called unto him, and said, Of what city art thou? And he said, Thy servant is of one of the tribes of Israel. And Absalom said unto him, See, thy matters are good and right; but there is no man deputed of the king to hear thee. Absalom said moreover, Oh that I were made judge in the land, that every man who hath any suit or cause might come unto me, and I would do him justice! And it was so, that when any man came nigh to him to do him obeisance, he put forth his hand, and took him, and kissed him." (II Samuel 15:2–5)

During the close of David's reign, his age and aloofness opened the door to opportunists like his very own son, Absalom. He seduced the hearts of Israel by feigning his father incompetent. He was committing something which happens in ministry quite often, the **spirit of patricide**. This is when the offspring seeks to kill the parent. As we mentor sons and daughters in the gospel and God begins to showcase them, ambitious pride and greed can set in and soon plots to displace the spiritual father crop up. Generally there is a following as in Absalom's case. This, of course, is rebellion and will be met with the judgment of God. It is better to leave than to commit the sin of patricide.

Another spirit roams the church, called the **spirit of infanticide**. This spirit enters the parent and causes them to murder the child. Many leaders have fallen prey to this spirit once they recognize God raising up a son or daughter in the midst and they do not embrace the process. Saul fell prey to this. David was like a son to him, but instead of nurturing, Saul sought to slay him. The **matricidal spirit** is the killing of the first lady. Not a few leaders' wives have left the ministry or had nervous breakdowns as they were attacked by others with criticism, rejection and harassment.

There is something called "the changing of the guard," where the son is ready to replace his father and mentor, as in the case of Elijah and Elisha. In such a case, God will speak to both parties involved, so that the transition can be made smoothly. The element of pride causes so much conflict in church leadership. May God help us in recognizing the pride in our own lives and eradicating it through the Word and the power of the Cross.

Absalom stole the hearts of Israel by subtly undermining of David's ministry. When Absalom is in the congregation, you'll hear things like:

"Let's pray for the pastor that he be more led of the Spirit."

"I could be up there if the pastor would give me a chance."

"Man, I have some dynamite ideas to help this church but the pastor won't listen to me."

"The service should have gone in a whole different direction, but the pastor is hindering the Spirit's move."

We had a brother who fell sway to the Absalom spirit. He went stealthily about the congregation taking a poll of those who disliked me or had been hurt by me. Needless to say, he found quite a crowd. He stroked their petty complaints and wooed their immaturity with, "Oh, he shouldn't have said that, we have to do something." He even went to the home of one family and gave money to the children. (You talk about buying votes). Finally, a meeting was summoned with all the wounded in attendance. A signed petition detailing their grievances and my ineptness was to be submitted to Dr. Farrell. One sister refused to sign, literally washing her hands of the whole deal. God used her to break the entire conspiracy as each one backed out and the rebellion was squashed. I learned of the details many years later.

The key to keeping rebellion down is to establish public policies based from the Word of God within the congregation. Policies like:

1. We never talk against headship in this church (Acts 23:5).
2. We take any conflicts to the proper party without involving anyone else (Matthew 18:15–17).
3. Anyone sowing discord in the congregation will be marked and avoided (Romans 16:17).
4. Anyone bringing division in the congregation will be warned twice, then asked to leave (Titus 3:10).

Chapter 25

SOUL TIES

"And man became a living soul." (Genesis 2:7)

A soul tie speaks of an adjoining or connection of the soul of one person with another person, place or thing. It is a literal bonding of the soul with someone or something else. The term soul tie is first referred to in the book of Genesis, Chapter 2, concerning the union between Adam and Eve. God made man a tripartite being and gave him the ability to become united in spirit, soul and body. In matrimony, once the marriage is consummated, God sees the two people as one flesh. Below I have listed some divine soul ties.

6 Divine Soul Ties

1. **Marital**—*"The two shall be one flesh."* Once holy matrimony occurs, God looks at the two as one. This is an acceptable soul tie. Notice that Adam and Eve were physically tied together. This was made possible because they were of the opposite gender. Same sex soul ties formed through sexuality is absolutely forbidden.
2. **Friendship**—*"And it came to pass, when he had made an end of speaking unto Saul, that the soul of Jonathan was knit with the*

soul of David, and Jonathan loved him as his own soul. . . . Then Jonathan and David made a covenant, because he loved him as his own soul" (I Samuel 18:1–3; 20:17). Here we have a perfectly acceptable soul tie between friends.

3. **Parental**—"*Now therefore when I come to thy servant, my father, and the lad is not with us; seeing that his life is bound up in the lad's life; It shall come to pass, when he seeth that the lad is not with us, that he will die*" (Gen. 44:31). Here, Judah is pleading for the return of his baby brother who is held captive in Egypt. Having already lost one son, the loss of another would be the end of Jacob because of his soul tie with Benjamin.

4. **Ministerial**—"*As they ministered to the Lord, and fasted, the Holy Ghost said, Separate me Barnabas and Saul for the work unto which I have called them*" (Acts 13:2). The Holy Ghost sent Barnabas and Saul forth in a pair. This is an example of a ministerial soul tie.

5. **Body of Christ**—". . . *but God hath tempered the body together, having given more abundant honor to the part which lacked*" (I Cor. 12:24). Once we are born again, we are baptized into one Body called the Body of Christ. Each member is tempered or knitted together by the same spirit.

6. **God**—"*What? Know ye not that your body is the temple of the Holy Ghost who is in you, whom ye have of God, and ye are not your own?*" (I Corinthians 6:19). The highest union between God and man occurs when we are filled with the Spirit. It is referred to as the baptism in the Holy Ghost. From the beginning God wanted to indwell man and be permanently tied to him.

Ungodly Soul Ties

"And Dinah, the daughter of Leah, whom she bore unto Jacob, went out to see the daughters of the land. And when Shechem, the son of Hamor the Hivite, prince of the country, saw her, he took her, and lay with her, and defiled her." (Genesis 34:2)

Dinah's case is particulary alarming because she represents so many women in this generation. She was a product of her father's disobedience. God told Jacob to return to Pandanaram, the land of his home, but he settled among the Canaanites in Shalem. Dinah innocently took a stroll out into the neighborhood, uncovered by her eleven brothers. This was her first mistake. Since the fall, God has given women a covering for their own safety. In this scenario, it was her brothers who would serve as her protectors.

She captivated the eye of Shechem, a Canaanite and he violated her in a moment of passion.

A soul tie resulted:

> "And his soul clave unto Dinah, the daughter of Jacob, and he loved the damsel, and spoke kindly unto the damsel. . . . And Hamor spake with them, saying, The soul of my son, Shechem, longeth for your daughter; I pray you give her him as his wife." (vv.: 3,8)

Sexual intercourse, forced or consensual, causes a bonding between the individuals involved. This explains why God ordained sexual intimacy to be practiced within the confines of marriage and marriage alone. A bonding between the spirit, soul, and body occurs during sexual intercourse which constitutes one of the many mysteries of creation.

Dinah was not only raped, but abducted and held captive until wedding arrangements could be made between the two fathers. Deception, mayhem and mass murder followed because of this heinous act. A terrible reproach was brought upon all of Israel. By the time God moved in, the entire family had fallen into idolatry and a serious house cleaning was needed before they could advance.

AHAB AND JEHOSHAPHAT

The league between Ahab and Jehoshaphat represents ungodly soul ties in the book of Kings. Ahab was a wicked ruler, racing toward judgment, and Jehoshaphat was the good, but misguided king of Judah. Their union was not only unhealthy and unholy, it was downright dangerous for Jeshoshaphat. God nonetheless spared the King of Judah while executing judgment on Ahab. There will be people in the Body of Christ who will be out of sorts with God and want to attach themselves to us. We must be careful not to tie in with them. Everyone on the ship destined for Tarshish was in jeopardy because Jonah was aboard. God's leading is paramount when it comes to relationships.

At the time of my conversion at Irvine, Carolyn was the first soul tie that God broke. Instinctively, I knew the relationship was over. No one had to tell me. I broke it without looking back, for nothing would have stunted my spiritual growth more than an ungodly relationship.

Since understanding the soul tie principle, I recall meeting people whom I just couldn't bond with. Though we are to love everyone, especially those of the household of faith, we do not tie into everyone, for not everyone is sent into our lives for a purpose. This does not mean they are evil. I remember when Holly came to Canton, two sisters wanted to get acquainted. She mentioned that she didn't feel comfortable around them. They were Jezebel and her clone. I had never spoken a word about them to Holly. She discerned their deceit, despite their compliments and smiles. When one called to arrange a friendly visit, Sister Johnson had a vision of the sister with a web covering her face. It was a symbol of Jezebellian cloning.

Samson and Delilah

Samson and Delilah are two obviously bad soul ties. Though Samson slew hundreds with his strength, he was reduced to a piece of bread by the insufferable badgering of Delilah. Bread is made from wheat that has been thrashed, ground, sifted and baked. Samson was brought to an embarrassing defeat by her. One thing the Lord showed me: Delilah was responsible for taking Samson's vision. So it is with any one of us who hook up with ties not ordained by God: it results in lost vision. Without vision in the Christian walk and especially in ministry, we perish. Vision is second only to life.

Our vision may have been shipwrecked by a wrong relationship, be it marriage, friendship, business, but all is not lost. God is a God of a second chance. You can make a comeback, even as Samson did.

Family Soul Ties

Since the family is the spawning bed for our physical and emotional growth, nothing will influence us more negatively or positively than family ties. Parents are put into our lives to love, guide, nurture and point us into the direction of our God. However, once we know God as Father, He must take hold of the reins of our lives and determine our course of divine destiny. In Matthew 10:34, Jesus speaks of destroying ungodly family soul ties.

> "Think not that I am coming to send peace on earth; I came not to send peace, but a sword. For I am come to set a man at variance against his father, and the daughter against her mother, and the daughter-in-law against her mother-in-law. And a man's foes shall be they of his own household."

How well we are loved before we are saved. We may be the household clown or the praise of the family, but let us get saved and love Him more than our family. Resentment may rise like a tide which precedes a typhoon. There may be a great difference between the saved and the unsaved, the consecrated and the unconsecrated, those who love Him and those who merely want to go to heaven, within the same household. Notice, the friction will not be only among the saved and the unsaved, but believers of the same faith and who attend the same church.

Nothing can describe the pain involved in God breaking a family soul tie. We must merely trust God and walk in the spirit as we are ripped, torn apart, persecuted, scorned, rejected, abandoned, smitten by those who once loved and highly esteemed us. The greater the call upon one's life, the greater this process will be. The key is to walk in love and wisdom. If the persecution comes from the parents, submit yourself and honor them regardless. God will defend you. He will not allow you to be destroyed. If you fall into rebellion, you become uncovered. You will fall into sin by breaking His commandments. The consequences can be devastating.

> "Children obey your parents in the Lord: for this is right. Honor thy father and mother (which is the first commandment with promise), That it may be well with thee, and thou mayest live long on the earth." (Ephesians 6:1–2)

I've counseled countless young converts broken in spirit by this process. We offer them comfort and direction but the process is God's dealing. We will never reign with Him unless we also suffer with Him. Nobody can hurt us more than our family. Yet God establishes Himself as the new parent in our lives. He breaks the old so that the new may be established. In time, He will mend every relationship if we allow Him to, but it will never be as it once was.

In earlier days at Deeper Life, many young people were tossed out of their homes by parents unable to deal with their new found love. The dramatic change dumbfounded the family and they attacked. Behind it all was God reconfiguring family relationships with a sword.

> "While he yet talked to the people, behold, his mother and his brothers stood without, desiring to speak with him. Then one said unto him, Behold, thy mother and thy brethren stand without, desiring to speak with thee. But, he answered and said unto him that told him, Who is my mother? and who are my brethren? And he stretched forth his hand toward his disciples, and said, Behold, my mother and my brethren! For whosoever shall do the will of my Father, who is in heaven, the same is my brother, and sister, and mother." (Matt.12: 46–50)

Earlier, I mentioned my wife's deliverance from family ties. The soul tie went much deeper than family relationships. Remember, a soul tie can extend to countries, locals, cultures, objects, rituals, fetishes, and the list goes on. Whatever the soul wraps itself around in undying devotion becomes a soul tie.

Naturally homesick when she arrived, it seemed that every other word she spoke was about England. American food was not like English food: our soda was not as strong, our cheese too weak, chocolate less sweet, potato chips lacked variety, and our tea was pale in comparison to British tea (which I couldn't argue with). After two years, she and our two children went to England for a two month visit. It was a dreadful decision for both of us. I could scarcely stand being in our new house alone. Telephone calls made it even worse. I had come a long way from loving solitude.

I flew over to get my family and when we returned, Alva said, "After a few weeks of seeing Mom and Dad, I was ready to come back. I realized that my purpose is beside my husband in the ministry in Canton." The soul tie was broken. Very few references were made to her homeland after that.

SOUL TIES AND THE ENTERTAINMENT WORLD

God showed me that there is a transference of spirits through the medium of popular music such as rock, gangster rap, hip-hop, and pop. Music stars are idolized by youth worldwide. Their continual exposure to music and movie videos releases a spiritual force that transforms their character. Violent lyrics beget violent behavior; suicidal lyrics promote the thoughts of suicide; blues music produces melancholia; sensual lyrics inspire lustful thoughts and actions.

More extreme cases occur when young people seek to become like their idols. During the early seventies a pop icon had many young male imitators going under the surgeon's knife to reconfigure facial features. They wanted to resemble his surgically altered face. The Bible makes it clear that we are to be transformed into the image of Christ. The world will forever worship the creature rather than the Creator. The church must not fall into the trap of self absorption. In fact, the current plastic surgery craze is fueled by a demon spirit. The devil is driving people into an unhealthy emphasis on the flesh. There is a fountain of youth, but not on this earth. It comes from drinking from the well of eternal life.

Prayer vigils and memorials are annually held by masses at the estate and gravesite of dead icons such as Elvis Presley and Marilyn Monroe, even though they contributed nothing particularly significant to society. Jesus told one disciple who asked permission to bury his father, *"Let the dead bury their dead; but go thou and preach the kingdom of God"* (Luke 9:60). Again, it is the diversion of the enemy to place the attention on the fallen flesh. It is a modern form of idolatry. We begin to focus on the first Adam at the expense of beholding the second Adam. The Bible makes it clear that the eye is the window to the human soul. Whatever we behold directly influences the mind, will and emotions. Unduly focusing on a person, despite their talent or beauty, creates a transforming effect into the image of that person. This is idolatry and sin. We are to be transformed into the image of Christ alone; however, we must behold Him (II Corinthians 3:18).

Having heroes for our children is not sinful. God elevates individuals for His glory and shows the world what He can do with a life. Those who live exemplary lives are excellent role models and ought to be undergirded with prayer. Those who live in sin need prayer as well, but their example should be shunned.

Jezebelic Soul Ties

Jezebel spins a web around those she uses to manipulate and control. Once they are her captives, they will lie, cover up, become human shields for her. As I said, their staunch loyalty toward her was a mystery to me until I realized that it was governed by the power of witchcraft.

The cloning can run deep also. The word clone in Webster's Collegiate Dictionary means, "to produce a copy or imitation, a person or thing that duplicates, imitates, or closely resembles another in appearance, function, etc." I have witnessed Jezebelic ties so deeply entrenched that though they sat several pews behind one another, two women literally made the same head gestures, facial expressions (mainly frowns) simultaneously. They even dressed alike.

Frequently while preaching, God has shown me an arch connecting two people in a service to indicate a soul tie in development, or similar shared character traits.

SYMPTOMS OF BAD SOUL TIE INFLUENCES

Below we list some telltale signs of bad soul ties. Though we all are influenced by others who come across our paths or whose lives we read about, a bad soul tie becomes a manipulation or unhealthy influence based on a connection. Here are some symptoms:

1. A person calls you on the phone to talk and immediately there's a negative mood shift, depression or anger at someone else.
2. We begin to develop a co-dependency upon others, seeking their directions on the least little thing.
3. The feeling of obligation to make ourselves accountable to those who are not our coverings such as our mates, employers, and our spiritual heads.
4. A feeling of being manipulated by others without power to resist them.
5. A need to report our actions, deeds, moves, dreams to someone other than our covering as listed in # 3.
6. A feeling of terror when corrected or rebuked by someone other than our appointed coverings listed in #3.
7. God sends people into our lives to build us up, correct us, impart knowledge and teach us. A bad soul tie will drain us and lead us to pettiness or unrighteous behavior.

SOUL TIES AND OUR YOUTH

Young people are particularly vulnerable to soul ties formed out of peer pressure. If a young lady associates with girls who are sexually active, she is likely to become sexually active too. If a young lady has friends who are teen mothers, look out, the spirit of promiscuity and early motherhood can be transferred. I've personally counseled several mothers who said that all their daughters' friends had out-of-wedlock babies. I warned them about the associations. I advised them to even forbid their daughters to go to the baby shower. Buying a gift is fine and appropriate, but teenage motherhood is not a celebration! In each case, these mothers turned out to become young grandmothers, despite my warnings. The power of soul ties is serious.

Gang influences pose a particular danger to our young men. Gangs are usually headed by a nest of demons influencing young men without male authority in their lives. They are grasping for manhood. The devil offers them lawlessness and drives them to initiate as many as they can. Driven by the need to belong and the specialness of acceptance, young men are sucked into a life of crime, drugs and violence. Hardened by the world influences of the music in this generation and their outward environment, they are plunged into a life of darkness and despair. As the spirit of dominion invades an area, entire neighborhoods are terrorized by gang activity. Safety on the streets becomes a byword. Killing becomes the norm.

Only the church has the answer to the mayhem and systematic self-destruction of our young males. When more prisons are constructed faster than universities, we are in trouble. Our help will not come from Capitol Hill, but Mount Zion. God must give us the strategy and the power to harvest this ripe group who, if turned around by His grace, could serve as a militant force against the one who once held them captive. If the church would turn down our plates and fast, replace our fashion show apparel with sackcloth, turn from our wicked ways and seek His face for the end time strategy, we would see a marvelous move from Him. He longs to do it.

Soul Ties and Deliverance

One day I counseled a young man in my apartment concerning marital and ministerial woes. He had a tremendous ministry as a preacher and prophet, but was estranged from his wife due to his infidelity. As we prayed, the Lord showed me that he was yet being unfaithful to Him in areas of sexual matters.

After leading him into a prayer of repentance, I had him renounce every relationship he had with women other than his wife (those he could remember). I bound the spirit of adultery and began to break sexual soul ties that kept him philandering. He trembled as I, by faith, called forth a virgin spirit within him—one undefiled by past relationships. With a shriek he collapsed prostrate on the floor and wept uncontrollably.

Soon after he left, I felt a pain in my stomach similar to a bad case of indigestion. I rarely get stomach aches so I was puzzled. The pain intensified, bowing me over until I fell on the couch in a fetal position. As it grew worse, I began to pray until I fell asleep. Upon waking the pain was gone. God revealed to me weeks later that it was retaliation of the demons that had been cast out. Soul ties that kept this man in adultery were broken and the devils were angry. I realized that deliverance is no joke. Demons are vindictive and we must remain under the blood covering always.

I realized from this and other incidents that everyone whom we've been intimate with becomes a part of us. When an individual has multiple sexual partners, the spirit of lust begins an endless search for gratification. Society applauds the male, but shuns the woman who falls into the lap of lust. In many cases we have had to set a person free from every sexual soul tie that they've had in order that the spirit can be presented before God as a virgin.

On an even darker note, we've had deliverance sessions with males who have had contact with animals. In one incident a young man came to the altar after noonday prayer and whispered that he was struggling with lust. We laid hands on him and he began to spit up globs of mucus immediately, before falling to the floor. Suddenly, his rear end lunged upward and he began bouncing around on his face and toes in a right angled position. I knew that this was the manifestation of a spirit of bestiality. Others were nearby so I firmly commanded the spirit of perversity to come out and it came out. After the session we went to my apartment to talk and I asked him if he had been involved in this sin and he affirmed the fact that he had.

This issue gets even murkier. In another case, a brother viewed bestiality on a pornographic banner on his computer. Never entering the web site, the mere glance at the banner opened the door to this spirit. The eyes truly are the windows of the soul.

Chapter 26

THE SIGHTLESSNESS OF SAMSON

"And the Lord answered me, and said, Write the vision, and make it plain upon tables, that he may run that readeth it. For the vision is yet for an appointed time, but at the end it shall speak, and not lie; though it tarry, wait for it, because it will surely come, it will not tarry."

"Then the Lord replied: write down the revelation and make it plain on tablets so that a herald may run with it, For the revelation awaits an appointed time; it speaks of the end and will not prove false. Though it lingers, wait for it; it will certainly come and will not delay." (Habakkuk 2:2–3 KJV / NIV)

"I therefore so run, not as uncertainly; so fight I, not as one that beateth the air;" (I Corinthians 9:26)

In August of the year 2000, I had the opportunity to address the entire Deeper Life Full Gospel Ministries with all its representing ministers on the island of Antigua. The Antiguan church was celebrating thirty years of existence. Progress had been made, but the pastor was desperate to hear from God concerning the destiny of the Deeper Life Ministries. I had been pastoring for thirteen years in Canton with little fruit. It was frustrating. I, too, was desperate. God had to give us all direction.

As I prayed, all I could get was the Book of Judges. I knew it was concerning Samson. I sighed and allowed God to minister the message to me. I was greatly humbled at what I learned and was compelled to share it.

Samson was a miracle baby born to childless parents. Consecrated from the womb for divine service, his parents received specific instructions on dietary habits and their son's Nazirite vow, which meant that no razor could come near his hair. Manoah and his wife believed and obeyed God and brought forth a judge for Israel with an unprecedented ministry of working miracles. Moses, Elisha, Elijah all had the working of miracles ministry, but none bore the mark of uniqueness as Samson. For the first time in Biblical history, God's anointing came upon a man and caused him to possess supernatural strength by which miracles would occur. Through this unusual but mighty ministry, his parents were told that, *"he shall begin to deliver Israel out of the hand of the Philistines"* (Judges 13:5).

Early on in his ministry, Samson showed a sad lack of consecration. In Chapter 14, we see him strolling in a vineyard in Timnah, a Philistine city. While there's nothing wrong with a vineyard in itself, the key here is what vineyards produce: grapes. Grapes were the main source of wine. Wine was one of the restrictions given to Samson's pregnant mother. If strong drink was forbidden to him as a fetus, then as a servant, he would be equally restricted. There is no clear evidence that Samson was a winebibber; however, his conduct clearly revealed that he would walk on the outer edge of his ministry.

While in this vineyard he crossed paths with a lion, whom he miraculously slew with his bare hands. Days later, Samson discovered that a swarm of bees had nestled in the lion's carcass and produced honey. Samson tasted the sweet honey and even took some home to his parents to eat. This was bad sign number two. Honey is fine, but it was extracted from an unclean beast, another restriction for his mother during her pregnancy.

From this, along with his mixed marriage, riddles and bantering with the Philistines, it was evident that Samson never took his ministry seriously. He never saw the greatness of his calling or his office as judge. Scores of men and women would line up from here to eternity to receive one ounce of what Samson played with: the miracle anointing of God. This was the beginning of Samson's end.

By the time we get to Chapter 16, Samson was a young widower, cavorting with a harlot. The anointing did not leave him, because it was not based on morality but upon consecration. The irony is that one cannot remain consecrated without possessing morals, hence, Samson's downfall was inevitable. The anointing is not easily obtained, nor forfeited; however, if we fail to maintain our consecration, we will see ourselves depleting. After one rendezvous with a harlot at Gaza, Samson took the gates of the city along with its bars. What a waste of the anointing that was supposed to break the yoke of the Philistines from off Israel's neck.

In the same chapter, Samson met his match, Delilah. Through cunning seduction, she pried the secret of his strength from him. There are some things about us and our ministries that no one needs to know. A tree consists of three main parts: roots, trunk, and branches. The trunk and branches are visible to all, but the root is the key to the life of the tree and is hidden to the naked eye. Without the root, all else would wither and die and yet it is the part that is not seen. Every minister must have a history, a secret life rooted in God, that no one knows. The measure in which we reveal our roots will determine the measure in which we will suffer loss. Samson made a costly mistake by telling the mystery behind his supernatural strength.

Soon after divulging the secret to his strength, Delilah betrayed him, placed him in a barber's chair and was laughing all the way to the bank. It was the Philistines, not Delilah, who shaved his head and put out his eyes. When I saw that, I felt that God was telling me that Samson was experiencing that which he always lacked: **vision**. The Philistines just made it a physical reality.

When we lack vision for our ministry, Delilah will come. She comes in so many forms for so many servants of God. She is not merely sensuality. For some, Delilah is success gone overboard. In Jim Bakker's autobiography, he spoke candidly of how PTL got so prodigious that it replaced prayer, consecration, fasting and sadly enough, his call to walk in holiness before the Lord. God was replaced with a high tech manufactured glory and well-polished entertainment. It was all fueled by an insatiable appetite for earthly success, but Ichabod ("inglorious") was written on the doorposts. The empire crumbled and became extinct.

Delilah can also be discouragement. When we lose our vision, we lose our way and wind up like Samson, grinding at a mill. The mill consisted of two large stones, one lay flat, while the other lay upon it upright with a pole attached. Generally, yoked oxen were fastened to the upright stone and walked in a circle as the grain was crushed beneath its weight. Samson had become a beast of burden, going in circles. I have known the depths of despair based on this portrait of Delilah.

For others, Delilah is an addiction: alcohol, drugs, nicotine, and unlawful sexual gratification. Unless these appetites are brought to Calvary, they will shear every lock that we have upon our heads. Secrecy is not a reality in the Kingdom of God. Moses made it plain, *"You can be sure, your sin will find you out"* (Numbers 32:23). We cannot hide who we are from God, nor from God's servants, particularly the prophets. However, though the prophet sees, that doesn't give him a license to judge an erring servant because God is able to make him stand in the end (Romans 14:4). The key here is that we must have ministry for ministers. God calls the imperfect into His service. We must have stations where ministers can get counseling and compassion without being destroyed for being a lump of clay carrying the glory of God.

Vision is everything. Without it, we perish. It is terrible to have a gift or a talent but have no vision for it. It will never rise to its fullest potential nor will you. Again, poor Samson lost sight of his vision (purpose) because he never recognized the greatness of his ministry. As God began to show me this in the scripture, I sank into deep repentance. I was Samson in dire need of a sanctified eye salve. I had allowed the hurt and abandonment of my earlier years as a pastor to wound me into the lap of utter discouragement.

I had lost sight of everything God had said. Though I would lip sync the vision to the congregation in Canton, I had never embraced it with a whole heart because my heart had been so broken. Therefore, the ministry could only go in a circular motion and not forward. I shuddered at my failure. I could not see the victory for seeing the surrounding area and the people it produced. I thought that without the right people there could be no victory, when true victory comes from God. He needs only to speak and it is done, whether we see it not. It takes faith.

Not only had I lost faith in God's promise, gone was my whole sense of self worth. The thought of anyone wanting to hear me teach or preach was incomprehensible. I shunned the very idea of radio or television because I thought I had nothing to offer. After all, my church was three quarters empty and had been that way for thirteen years. Who would want to hear what I had to say? I had been beaten down. With no keepers of the flame, and giants in all the land, I had silently acquiesced and been lulled to sleep in Delilah's lap. There was no more fight left in me. I merely existed. The darkness was deep, the enemy was closing in and I was probably as close to God as any sinner would be.

The next thing God showed me is another mistake Samson made. Samson begot no sons or daughters after himself, spiritually. No one was able to catch the mantle, no one was mentored to stand in the office of judgeship after his reign. As a result, we see lawlessness and decadence as never before recorded in the history of Israel. One could hardly believe that Chapters 17–20 were part of the Holy Writ, but they are. They are there to show us what happens when leaders lose their vision and fail to mentor others to carry on the vision.

I listed the mistakes that Samson made throughout his ministry:

1. Failure to consecrate himself to God. (Samson cried out to God only twice, both times when he was in trouble.)

2. Failure to maintain a moral life. (If we are one thing behind the pulpit and another behind closed doors, we are heading for an embarrassing fall.)
3. Poor choice of marriage. (Nothing will affect ministry more than our mates.)
4. Failure to see the seriousness of his call to devastate the Philistines. (Every call to divine service is vital, whether it is to the healing ministry or to keep the doors of the church.)
5. Flippant and frivolous nature. (Samson lacked godly character which comes from discipline of the Holy Ghost.)

Samson clowned throughout his ministry and now, in the last episodes of his life, the joke was not on him, but the joke was him! He had been reduced to a buffoon, a court jester, and a laughingstock. Though his mistakes were numerous and costly, the Philistines made the greatest mistake of all. They let Samson live. They should have killed him. But because they did not know the scripture nor the power of God, they doomed their own souls by this single act of ignorance and arrogance.

> "He giveth power to the faint; and to those who have no might he increaseth strength." (Isaiah 40:29)

They did not know that God was a merciful God. They did not know that God would toss our sins in a sea of forgetfulness. They didn't know that in the prison Samson's hair was growing back (a sign of resurrection.)

Micah has some verses that I could imagine were the sentiments of Samson's heart as he asked the lad to take him to the pillars.

> "Rejoice not mine enemies when I fall, I shall arise. And when I sit in darkness, the Lord shall be light for me." (7:8)

Here Samson was alone and friendless. Delilah had deserted him. The Philistines mocked him. Israel rejected him. He had no one to turn to but God. He had nothing else to do but to align himself with purpose and then push. No amount of earthly pleasure or accomplishment can become a fulfilling substitute for the purpose that God placed us upon the earth. Only what we do for Christ will meet us in eternity.

As I preached this message, I called on the audience in Antigua to help me push. As they cried "push" in succession, I called out greatness to come forth out of the Deeper Life Ministries. I called for books to be published, songs produced, a training center to be built, auditoriums to be filled, kings and world leaders to witness the work God had wrought in this ministry. I decided that God would get the glory, be it by my life, or by my death. I could not return to Canton the same preacher.

I've shared this painful chapter of my life with anyone who has failed God. I give you a charge, "Put your hands to the pillars and push." God saw that divorce, that moral failure, that felony, that out-of-wedlock pregnancy, that scandal, that fatal blow from the enemy that sent you careening off course, before you were placed in your mother's womb. Yet, He still called you. He still predestined you to do what He equipped and anointed you to do. Push. Don't worry about the wagging tongues, or the jeers of the enemy. Don't focus in on the rejection from the church. Don't look at your failures or sins, but look unto Jesus, the Author and Finisher of the race you are foreordained to win. Get up and push.

Samson pushed his way back into purpose and ended in Hebrews, Chapter 11, the hero's hall of faith. There is no mention of his failure there, only his faith. King David is there too, along with Moses, Gideon, and Rahab. Whereas people judge our life's failures and past reputation, God goes beyond judging our sin—He judges our faith. Without it, you cannot please Him. For God is a God who is greater than any failure we could commit. So push with all **your** might.

I returned to Canton not ready to get busy, but ready to lie before God to renew my vows. Relationship precedes work. Many of God's servants are busy doing the work of the Lord without knowing the Lord of the work. This becomes the launching pad of failure. I had to renew covenant fellowship first, then get busy with the strategy to elevate the Deeper Life Ministries. I felt my strength returning. I could face the future with optimism once again. I was ready to be a leader, ready to write the vision so that he who read it could run with certainty, and he who would fight could do so without shadow boxing. We, as a church, were well able to take down the giants in Canton. They were indeed bread for us. The victory had already been won by faith two thousand years ago by the obedience of one man. It felt marvelous to be back on track. Bless the name of the crucified Lamb, Jesus the Christ!

Epilogue

Years ago when I was home on Christmas vacation from Irvine, I went to the home of a preacher named Reverend Brunner. Ironically, I was gathering information for a book I was writing on my life. I was unsaved at the time, but I have always had a burning desire to write. I was told that Reverend Brunner had a key element to a piece of family history, so I arrived unannounced, and was welcomed into his immaculate home just a block down from Lathrop Elementary School on the Southeast end of Canton.

I was disappointed as he had no information to give, but he told me that he was impressed with my character and candor. I was buttoning my coat to depart into crisp winter air when he posed a question.

"Young man, what are you really looking for?" he asked.

"I'm looking for truth," I said in my usual confident tone.

With that, he reached for a huge Bible sitting opened on the coffee table.

"Read this verse," he commanded.

"*In the beginning was the Word and the Word was with God and the Word was God*" (John 1:1).

He flipped to another passage in the same book, pointed to the bold print and told me to read.

"*Sanctify them with thy truth, thy word is truth*" (John 17:17).
"Now, what was in the beginning," he asked?
"The Word," I responded.
"And what is the Word?"
"God," I answered in a classroom voice.
"And what is truth?"
"The truth is the Word . . . and the Word was in the beginning . . . and the Word was God . . . so the truth is . . . God" I said as if a bomb had gone off inside my mind!
"You're a fine young man. You'll find the Truth someday," he said with a confident smile.

I felt that I had stumbled upon a treasure chest of knowledge. The Truth is God. Wow! I was blown away by this revelation. I learned that God was truth, He was light, He was love, and He was good. Whenever we walk in those elements: truth, goodness, love, and light, we transcend the world that we live in and walk as kings and conquerors on the earth. Just one act of goodness, one gesture of love, a spoken word of truth, and a walk in the revelation (light) of God, can revolutionize this earth. Gerald literally rebuked my wrath with one disarming statement of his love toward me. He carried a weapon more powerful than a Uzi within his mouth. I was smitten on the spot, destined for the portals of glory.

I was always bent on militancy and revolution. Now God had given me grounds for legitimate expression of each. I could be a radical for the kingdom of God: a militant with a message of love. And whether we see the end results of it or not, love never fails and evil is always swallowed up by good. My prayer is to walk in these truths as long as I live.

Valuable Lessons

I have had some super highs in God and some indescribable valley lows. Each time, God sought to teach me kingdom lessons, but often I was too bruised to get the message. Once I sobered up, I began to allow God to filter through the pain and give me substance in my suffering. One of the profound lessons was found in

His command to Joshua before entering into the Promised Land. *"Be strong and of good courage"* (Joshua 1:5). God exhorted Joshua three times this same way. Strength and courage are what we need most while pressing into the promised land. Courage is not the absence of fear. It is the victorious response to fear. It arises out of our spirit as a direct response to fear and terror. It comes from keeping our eyes fastened upon the Lord. As long as Peter looked at Jesus, he walked the raging sea. One glance at the billows and he sank with an anvil of fear about his neck. Courage is a God-inspired attribute.

Courage didn't exist in Eden before the fall. Adam was the landlord. He frolicked with lions, played with scorpions and wrestled with bears. But after the fall, not only did death enter into the picture but so did fear. Adam's first manifestation of fear was toward God Himself. This was not reverential honor, it was terror. He was literally terrified at the voice of God walking through the garden. God did not want man to walk in fear because it would nullify man's ability to have faith, so God gave Adam an antidote. It was courage. Again, courage is the victorious response to fear and terror.

Pastoring can become so overwhelming that our courage is zapped. While pursuing promises and fulfilling our purposes in life, many obstacles, frustrations, misses, will occur and it will require strength and courage to overcome them. Both are a result of keeping focused on the Lord. If we look at the winds of persecution, the waves of rebellion, the whispers, lies and betrayals, we will sink in despair. I have been guilty of it, and can vouch that it will halt your advancement. Three times God spoke strength and courage to Joshua. Every leader needs to heed this exhortation.

Eternal Rewards

God taught me another lesson while I was suffering from exhaustion and depression. After years of earnest labor and no income from the church, our church remained small and riddled with rebellion. The people whom God sent in were challenged in every area of life: financial, emotional, mental, marital, spiritual; so much so that hours of ministry was needed just to get them in the pews on Sunday mornings. Crack and drug addiction took most the brothers from the church back into the streets. Out-of-wedlock pregnancies removed many promising young ladies. Those who came into the ministry with spiritual stability were soon used by the spirits of Jezebel, Korah, or Absalom in an attempt to take over the ministry. I felt like I was wasting my life. I was sinking deeper in despair when the Lord came to me with this parable.

In essence He told me to consider a huge, brand new, retail toy store like Toys' R' Us in the suburbs and a small, dingy, second-hand toy shop in the inner city. Both managers have one objective: to get toys ready for that special day, be it birthday, Christmas, or other. The manager at Toys' R' Us has top of the line, designer toys; but the inner city manager must repair broken truck wheels, reattach heads on Barbie dolls, mend, sew, paint, polish, and glue toys that have been abused over the years. In the end, both toy stores are able to set their wares in the window for display. There are toys for the wealthy, but there must be toys for those who cannot afford high prices, for the poor you will have with you always (John 12:8). Both managers are hired by Him. One may have a bigger budget, a larger selection, and a more attractive inventory, but each will receive the same reward in the end if they remain faithful to their call.

I sighed and prayed for all inner city pastors and ministers. Those who have to work secular jobs; those who get 3:00 a.m. calls from suicidal parishioners; those who sleep in their churches Saturday night to keep the crack addicts from breaking in. I prayed for them and continue to pray for a special grace to deal with a special people who must learn that Jesus loves them and died for their sins and has a better life for them.

Again, the Lord gave me another example from the scriptures concerning His disciples. The Lord chose twelve, one of whom was a defector. Of the three closest to the Lord, James was martyred early in his ministry. Peter and John wrote epistles along with Matthew. Phillip received a miracle working and deliverance ministry. Of the rest, including Mathias, Judas' replacement, little is said about their ministry and work. Yet all were equally the Lord's disciples and had thrones reserved especially for them. If we judge our spiritual success on earthly standards, we will become either puffed up and fall into delusion, or dismayed by comparing our merits with others. The Bible clearly teaches us that they who compare themselves with themselves are not wise (II Corinthians 10:12).

NUMBERS

Another lesson occurred during my pastoral anniversary appreciation. I sat in the honored seat. As tributes were given, I scanned the empty pews. I recalled the tireless labor that had been rendered. I felt numb and a bit embarrassed. Then the Lord gave me a series of lessons in stages.

Bigger is not necessarily better. Today, huge congregations are the "in" thing for the Kingdom of God. Nevertheless, clearly every believer does not fit inside the mega church. Some need that small, intimate setting where they can be parented and nurtured by headship. A family setting is part of their healing. While we applaud and pray for those who are running congregations in the multiple thousands, let us not despise nor neglect the tremendous work going on in the storefronts. Let us not be like Eliab who snubbed his nose at his little brother and his *"few sheep"* (I Samuel 17:28). God honored David's faithful care of his tiny flock and was preparing him to rule a kingdom. Never despise the day of small beginnings.

Faithfulness over a few translates to rulership over many. For some pastors this means a full reward in heaven. It can also apply to natural blessings as well. God is preparing many inner city pastors for greatness. Storefronts can become auditoriums when God's spirit moves in our cities. The faithful pastor will abound in blessing. The process is undeniably painful but God uses trials and adversities to train, prune, and produce five star Generals. We shall certainly reap if we faint not.

When Gideon was ready to attack the Midianites with twenty-two thousand, God said reduce the numbers. The ranks fell to ten thousand. Gideon thought it a good number but God again reduced the ranks to three hundred. With these few, God gave Israel the victory. There are times when God will reduce to produce. If we are merely gloating over members, we will miss God.

Numbers impress us, but not God. King David numbered Israel and fell under the disciplinary hand of God. Jesus never changed His message to obtain or retain a crowd. Seventy disciples turned away when Jesus spoke about eating His flesh and drinking His blood in John, Chapter 6. I imagine they thought He was a cult leader, promoting cannibalism. After they left, the Lord turned to the twelve and asked, *"will you also go away?"* (v. 38). The Lord is concerned with quality more than quantity. You can churn out conquerors in a two hundred member church and pastor thousands and have nothing but a high tech Laodicia.

When John received the revelation, he saw a host in heaven which no man could number. Again, God could have given him the number, but it wasn't an important issue with Him. The important issue was that they were overcomers. God was teaching me that eternal rewards will not be based on "how many" but on "how well." How well we served Him. Did we do His will? Did we serve in holiness, sincerity, and truth? Did we keep the faith? Were we a keeper of the flame? Did we finish the work? If so, we will surely hear Him say, "well done."

Apologies to the Patriarchs

God showed me myself in and through the lives of many of the Patriarchs and Matriarchs of Old and New Testaments. I felt a need to apologize to some of them whom I had looked down upon. Though I did not actually speak out against them, I simply read their stories in a detached, didactic way. I judged them as being someone distinctly different from me. God helped me to realize that I, like many of them, have failed and come short of the glory

Epilogue

in some of the exact same areas. It is only His grace and mercy that brings any of us through.

My first apology goes to Peter. I, too, have stepped out into the deep things of God, only to sink amid the tempest when I took my eyes off of the Lord. It is easy to consider the whirling winds and boisterous waves above the Lord's call "to come." I must apologize for deriding him for his cowardly display just before the crucifixion. I, too, have denied Him when the heat was on and when it would cost me most.

Next, I bow humbly before Lot's wife. I have taken glances backward to sins, places, hurts, injustices and people from whom I was delivered. Unto my brother, Esau, I apologize because my fleshly appetites have caused me to esteem the things of God lightly upon occasion. An apology goes to Gideon for I, as he did, still wonder how on earth God would want to use me, the least of all the saints. I apologize to Phillip who walked with the Lord for three and a half years and did not know Him. I have walked with Him much longer and still do not recognize His power as I should. Unto Didymus Thomas whose faith I looked down upon while overlooking his courage. For it was Thomas who said, *"Let us go and die with Him"* (John 11:16). I apologize for I, too, have told the Lord that I could not believe except I see. I apologize to Elijah whom I loved until his flight in Chapter 17 of II Kings. I overestimated his humanity and underestimated the power behind Jezebel's wickedness. I, too, have run and hid away in a cave of obscurity at her threats.

What I realized is that we can never point the finger at anyone, ever, because we are likely to mirror their error in some form down the road, if we live long enough. Our criticism of others is rooted in either envy or pride or both. We can walk above this if we focus on Christ.

The Faithfulness of God

As a youngster, I remember having an Aunt Ida Mae promise us that she would take us to the beach one summer Saturday afternoon. I was ecstatic not only because I hadn't been before, but also because I thought beaches were only for the Frankie Avalon and Annette Funicello crowd.

Aunt Ida Mae was very sweet and an incredible beauty. With high cheek bones, and large doe-like eyes pasted on the backdrop of mahogany skin, one could not help but stare at her. Even more memorable than her beauty were her words.

As a devout Muslim, she spoke words of black pride rarely heard in our neighborhood in the sixties. She spoke of times when we were kings and queens and instilled in us an unmistakable sense of self worth. She was the first one to correct our entire family on calling the Brazil nut a "nigger toe." She said this was a negative connotation given to a perfectly innocent nut as a means of demeaning our race. We stopped using the term immediately because we had learned its proper name for the first time.

As I waited outside I knew that she would not disappoint us. When the first few hours passed, Bettie was off with a friend. I reminded her of the engagement and she said she didn't want to go. An hour later James left with his friends, leaving me and Kat waiting ever so expectantly. As the sun went down, Kat abandoned her post and went into the house, but not me. Aunt Ida Mae had promised us. She wouldn't break her promise. I held my ground, sitting on the pavement until the stars danced at the symphony of the crickets. I sadly left when Momma called me into the house to get ready for bed.

I can't determine whether my waiting was going to make the promise come to pass, or the promise had compelled me to wait so unswervingly, but I went to bed deeply disappointed. God brought this back to my remembrance not to recall the pain but to assure me that:

> "God is not a man that He should lie; neither the son of man that he should repent. Hath he not said, and shall he not do it? Or hath he not spoken, and shall he not make it good?" (Numbers 23:19)

Epilogue

Millennium Message

During our New Year's Eve's millennium service, I spoke to the congregation on a message that God gave, about trusting Him for the new century. Trusting God is only easy when you sing and read about it. Executing trust is another thing altogether. He broke down the meaning of trust with this acronym:

Taking
Rest
Under (the)
Sovereign
Testings (of God)

Trusting is more than a notion.

In every phase of my life I have had to wrestle with God, like Jacob did at Jabbok, until I would surrender and rest in His sovereign choosing. My first wrestling came when God asked me to forsake my dreams of being in show business and follow Him. I died that night. I had studied the arts for five years, struggled for a degree that was no longer suited for His purpose. I was devastated. He said He had a much better life in store, but I couldn't see it, I just had to trust Him.

My second major wrestling match with God was stepping into the pulpit behind Dr. Farrell. It was a really difficult transition but again faith plus a little fire, helped me make it through.

Marriage was a frontier that I wrestled with God. I was running for years and never understood His mind on the matter. I remember when I was going through the turmoil about being married God said, "Son, before you marry someone, you must first have a marriage with Me. It is a wedding of the will." I knew that I had to travail, wrestle, and die to self to make the transition from bachelorhood. Again through the power of faith and trust, I overcame this obstacle and plunged headlong into the blessings of the

Lord. Marriage has made all the years of suffering worthwhile. God was most gracious in giving me a wife like Alva.

In every major stage of my spiritual development, faith was required, faith in an invisible God. Faith in a God who does not fail His people. Everything that I know about deliverance could be put on the tip of the tiniest needle head with plenty of room left! It's pretty much the same when it comes to my knowledge of God and His Word. Yet the pursuit of knowledge is what makes this journey so fascinating. There is a sheer joy in discovering God and understanding who He really is. It is a joy that will never end even when we enter His eternal kingdom.

The Bible says that we go from strength to strength, faith to faith, and from glory to glory. In other words, despite our strength today, there is greater strength ahead for the journey. If we have faith to move mountains, there are planets to move, for faith is ever increasing as we exercise that which we already have. Finally, the endless glory of God awaits us; we need never be satisfied with a little touch from God, a vision or a dream. I've determined to press on, laying aside every weight and sin, while being careful to avoid striking the rock twice, producing an Ishmael, making a hasty vow, and strolling on the roof top when the battle is on. If I make a mistake (and they are inevitable), I will have to trust God just as Moses, Abraham, Jephthah and David did. They are all listed in Hebrews 11.

One unforgettable thing I've learned in my journey with God: the greatest work to be done here on earth lies not in our ability to produce mega churches, publications, CDs, massive outreaches, Christian villages for God; but it lies in the work that God can do in us by the power of the cross and the discipline of the Holy Ghost. We can become intoxicated by the external Babels that are built to give "us" a name. God wants to build in man specimens for His glory, men who have surrendered totally to His will and completely sold out. This is what happened to Enoch, and God took him. The church is yet to see what God can do with a man who has lost himself wholly in Him. He's still searching for the man with the perfect heart toward Him. I so desperately want to qualify.

God has taught me that we can be doing many great things in His name yet be living ninety percent of our lives in the flesh. That means a mere ten percent is actually yielded to the indwelling Holy Spirit. These are staggering percentages. Our aim in this generation is not to be visible, but available. John the Baptist came to preach the way, prepare the way, and then get out of the way. Upon seeing his cousin approaching the Jordan River, John proclaimed, "*He must increase, but I must decrease*" (John 3:30). In reference to His cousin, the Lord said, "*Among them that are born of women there hath not risen a greater than John the Baptist*" (Matt 11:11).

Greatness is not necessarily visibility. It is not the glory cloud around the tomb that validates us for ministry, but it is the blood stain around the cross that does. "*So then death worketh in us, but life in you,*" (II Corinthians 4:12). In the Old Testament God said, "*eye for eye, tooth for tooth, hand for hand, foot for foot*" (Exodus 21:24). Under the law if someone injured his brethren, it would cost him the same price as that which was lost. Thank God we are under grace and not under the law. However, God requires something deeper of us: a life for a life; that is, our (soulish) life for His resurrection life. This is the call of discipleship, the call to sell out. The church suffers for the lack of the exchange.

The cry to get all that you can from this earth dominates the air waves today. It is popular, but is it scriptural? We clearly know that God has freely given us all things on this earth to enjoy. We also know that God delights in the prosperity of His servants. Wealth is clearly part of the Abrahamic covenant in which we are all heirs by faith. However, God gives us warnings of the dangers of the power that money and the cares of this world can have upon us if we place our love upon them. Besides this, there is a prosperity demon that God showed me years ago, hence, we must stay balanced, scriptural, and focused on Him at all times. The key is that we may have things, as long as things do not have us.

I've learned that in Christ you can never be a loser, only a chooser. As long as you choose to go on in spite of your weakness and failures, setbacks, mess ups, and misses, you win. Just like I won the race at Wesleyan. Oh, the Greek fraternities laughed at us and said that we lost, but perseverance said we won. There is no indictment in placing last in a race, the indictment comes when we fail to finish the race. We won because we continued to run. Therefore I say unto you, the reader, run your race to win. Never give up. The real Winner inside of you crossed the finish line nearly 2000 years ago.

More importantly, I learned that the power of good is greater than the power of evil. Gerald proved this when he turned the other cheek as I smote him with my fury. It was as if his words sailed on the wings of a white dove that landed in my troubled heart, bringing it peace. I was wooed to God in one swoop. Truly we must never render evil for evil, but overcome evil with good.

In the meanwhile, battles must be fought if victories are won. We must tread on scorpions, take up serpents, and crush the black widow spider until the church is free from rebellion. Above all, lessons must be learned if we are to really know Him. Nothing really matters in life but loving people and knowing God. Such knowledge is full of pain and glory, triumphs and tribulations, just like the road to Calvary.

The apostle Paul put it this way, *"That I may know him, and the power of his resurrection, and the fellowship of his sufferings, being made conformable unto his death"* (Philippians 3:10). I am eternally indebted to God for what He has taught me thus far, which is but a smidgen of what lies ahead—as I embark upon new frontiers in the walk of faith, drink deeper from the well of His Word; flow higher in His anointing and take another step into the mysteries of the deliverance ministry.

Endnotes

1 Maya Angelou, Bantam Book / Random House, Inc. 201 E. 50th St. New York, N.Y. 10022

To order additional copies of

A Step Into
DELIVERANCE

Have your credit card ready and call

Toll free: (877) 421-READ (7323)

or send $14.95* each plus $4.95 S&H** to

WinePress Publishing
PO Box 428
Enumclaw, WA 98022

www.winepresspub.com

*WA residents, add 8.4% sales tax

**add $1.00 S&H for each additional book ordered

For more information about the author log onto:
www.deeperlifefullgospel.org

Or write:

DLFG
P.O. Box 9429
Canton, Ohio 44711-9429